UNDERSTANDING
NEW AGE
LIVING

Executive Editor: Jane McIntosh
Editor: Nicola Hodgson
Copy-editor: Mary Lambert
Creative Director: Keith Martin
Design Director: Mark Winwood
Designer: Les Needham
Picture Researchers: Wendy Gay and Denise Lalonde
Production Controller: Lisa Moore

First published in Great Britain in 2000
by Hamlyn an imprint of
the Octopus Publishing Group Limited,
2-4 Heron Quays, London, E14 4JP

Copyright © 2000 Octopus Publishing Group Limited

ISBN 0 600 59768 7

A CIP catalogue record for this book is available from
the British Library

Printed in China

NEW AGE LIVING

a guide to principles, practices
and beliefs

Paul Roland

hamlyn

CONTENTS

CHAPTER 1
Sacred Secrets

CHAPTER 2
Tuning in to Mother Earth

CHAPTER 3
Foreseeing the Future

CHAPTER 4
Soul Searching

CHAPTER 5
Inner child and Higher Self

CHAPTER 6
Holistic Health

INTRODUCTION

We live in an age of information overload, of intense competition and growing pressure to conform, where stress sets the pace by which many of us live our lives, so it is perhaps inevitable that an ever increasing number of people are turning to 'alternative' beliefs and complementary therapies in search of something that will bring them peace of mind, and give a sense of meaning to their lives. In fact, most people are searching for something that will answer the needs of their mind, body and spirit.

The meaning of life

At the beginning of the 21st century we have unlimited access to the accumulated knowledge of the ancient and modern world and yet, few of us can honestly say that we have a real understanding of what life is about, other than in terms of the obvious stages which define our development from infant to adult. The formulas, the facts and the theories of three millennia are ours for the asking, to be called up on screen at the touch of a button or studied at leisure on the printed page, but it would seem that their significance still eludes us.

The recent intensification of interest in the paranormal is an indication that our insatiable curiosity regarding our True Nature and innate abilities is undimmed. Unfortunately, much is being made of the phenomena themselves, and not the substance and significance of what they reveal of the greater reality beyond our physical world.

The scientific view

In their search for answers some people turn to science, but science too has its share of inexplicable phenomena, such as the anomalies of quantum theory and the recent discovery that the universe is continuing to expand in contradiction to the laws of physics. We have discovered the basic building blocks of life and can genetically manipulate these for our own ends, but the fundamental mysteries of life, the spark and its source, remain a mystery.

In spite of the miraculous advances in medical science which make the surgical procedures of 50 years ago seem primitive by comparison, we in the West still fall prey to illness, to infection and dis-ease, while a comparatively disproportionate number of people in the East appear to live longer and healthier lives.

For these reasons many in the West have become disenchanted with institutionalized religion, frustrated by what they see as conventional medicine's over-dependence on prescription drugs and dismayed at our wholesale disregard for the environment. But equally they are wary of the profusion of exotic alternatives which appear to offer easy answers, instant enlightenment and a quick fix.

'Alternative' practices

This book aims to dispel many of the myths and misconceptions shrouding these alternative practices and the principles which they embody. In doing so they are revealed to be the expressions of a shared esoteric tradition which encompasses such apparently diverse, but ultimately complementary concepts as karma and kabbalah, shamanism and spiritual healing, Tibetan Buddhism and the tarot. These are just a

Ancient monuments such as the temple of Kalasasaya in Bolivia and the Sphynx in Egypt indicate the existence of an advanced civilization pre-dating dynastic Egypt.

few strands of what is sometimes referred to as the 'golden thread' of the Ageless Wisdom which superstition and our blind faith in science has obscured for centuries.

One of the purposes of this book is to pull these tangled strands together so that you may feel more confident to choose the path or practice which is most suited to your needs and lifestyle. We tend to put all our efforts into one aspect of our lives: physical fitness, intellectual achievement or spiritual exploration, but the underlying message of all the traditions outlined in this book is that we have to treat ourselves holistically. For to ignore the needs of mind, body and spirit is to deny our true nature and that can cost us not only our health but also our sense of wellbeing and our love of life.

Our understanding of our true nature has been hampered by the belief that human evolution is a linear progression from the 'primitive' state to one of technological superiority, but it could be argued that technology has brought greater efficiency rather than insight and that our accumulation of knowledge has brought us no nearer to

understanding the nature of the world we inhabit nor the wisdom we need to live in harmony with it.

Recent discoveries in the field of archaeology seem to substantiate the claims for the existence of an advanced civilization predating dynastic Egypt by thousands of years whose 'lost knowledge' of the unifying principles of the universe we are only now rediscovering. And with it, perhaps, the essence of our humanity.

The aims of the book
The book is divided into six sections. In the first, entitled Sacred Secrets, the esoteric tradition and its secret teachings are traced from ancient Egypt to the secret societies and occult orders of more recent times, who each claimed to be custodians of the Ageless Wisdom. In the same section there is also a description of how to make your own Tattwa cards, which are symbols designed to help penetrate the unconscious mind. These are of Eastern origin but were part of the techniques used by the 19th century occult order The Hermetic Order of the Golden Dawn. This order and the

contemporary, The Theosophical Society, were largely responsible for introducing the central concepts of karma and reincarnation to the West. These still much misunderstood subjects are covered in the same section.

Of all the Eastern practices to be adopted by the West, Yoga must be the most widely practised, and although it aids mind, body and spirit, it is commonly perceived as a purely physical activity. As well as giving a description of the basic asanas, or postures, for you to try I have also briefly outlined the philosophy behind the practice. The section ends with a look at paganism and its modern expression, Wicca, which is currently the fastest growing religious movement in the USA.

The second section, titled Tuning In To Mother Earth, examines the idea that the planet is both a living being and a matrix of energy to which our ancestors were highly sensitive. It is known that our health can be adversely affected by living in the vicinity of overhead power cables or in a house which has been built over an underground stream, but it seems that the ancients may have had a deeper understanding of the invisible forces to which we are only now becoming gradually aware. The section ends with a look at the phenomenon of 'channelled' teachings and a summary of the prophecies and predictions made by the 'New Age' gurus including Alan Watts and James Redfield.

The third section, Foreseeing The Future makes what I consider to be a convincing case for the existence of precognition and the impressive record of accuracy and insight offered by such techniques as the tarot, runes, astrology, palmistry, scrying with a crystal ball and the I Ching. Again, from the descriptions given and a few sample exercises it is possible for anyone to test the claims for themselves and obtain a reasonably accurate reading for themselves, a friend or family member.

The fourth section, Soul Searching, probes deeper beyond the psyche to the spiritual realms to look at the wisdom of Buddhism, the nature of mystical experience, and techniques to stimulate altered states of consciousness. Exercises in 'pathworking', a form of creative visualization, and contacting angels are also included.

The fifth section, Inner Child and Higher self,

Above: Cave paintings such as the one above suggest that prehistoric man used magic to subdue the animals he wished to hunt.
Right: A shrine to a tree spirit in Ghana. Animism, or the belief that nature is alive with spirits, was the earliest expression of man's spirituality.

examines the enigma of the personality and includes exercises for awakening the Higher Self, dreamworking and reprogramming the unconscious mind using a form of hypnotherapy. From Gurdjieff to the popular personal growth gurus here is evidence that we all have the most powerful means of personal transformation within our grasp – our minds.

The final and largest section of the book is a comprehensive guide to the most common complementary therapies of East and West, from Ayurveda to psychic surgery, outlining which problems are suitable for treatment, the known benefits, and the reason why they have been proven effective.

This book is designed to be practical, all-inclusive and user-friendly, for all those seeking a positive, no-nonsense guide to developing greater self-awareness, health and general wellbeing.

The meditation and visualization exercises included in this book are designed for relaxation and developing self-awareness. However, anyone who has emotional or mental problems or who has had problems of this nature in the past should seek professional medical advice before attempting any of these exercises. The author and the publisher accept no responsibility for any harm caused by or to anyone as a result of the misuse of these exercises.

CHAPTER 1

SACRED SECRETS

One of the most important resources of New Age ideas, beliefs and practices is the body of knowledge known collectively as the Western esoteric tradition. This is a golden thread of arcane and ageless wisdom woven from Egyptian, Judaic and early Christian mystical doctrines and disciplines but it also incorporates the classical Mystery Religions and Greek philosophy. These apparently diverse traditions share a common holistic view of the world. According to this concept each human being is a microcosm, a universe in miniature, and through attuning ourselves to the natural forces around us we can master both our body and our mind and ultimately awaken the living God within.

To this has been added the central concepts of the Eastern esoteric tradition; karma, the transmigration of souls, the significance of the chakras and the practice of yoga, which is considered so important in maintaining health and vitality, and the search for personal enlightenment.

Dhankar monastery, Spiti, India

Egyptian mysteries

Egypt exercised a singular fascination for initiates of the occult schools of the 19th century and it continues to hold a fascination for those who believe that the ancients were custodians of a secret wisdom which people of today have lost through preoccupation with materialism.

In the Western esoteric tradition, Egypt is believed to be the fount, if not the source, of all knowledge concerning the nature of the self and of the universe which we are seeking to rediscover today.

For example, it is now known that the Egyptians identified the psyche and the spirit which they called the shadow (khabit) and the body of gold (sahu). Within the latter was to be found the soul (ba) and the Divine spark (khu), a unity which was symbolized in the custom of placing sarcophagi of increasing refinement within one another. The physical body was animated by a life force which the Egyptians called Ka (comparable with the prana of the Hindu tradition and the chi recognized by the Chinese) which initiates sought to channel during meditation for the purpose of raising their awareness.

Egyptian temples

The structural layout of Egyptian temples, specifically the temple at Luxor, is thought to symbolize the human anatomy, just as Jewish synagogues are designed to reflect the Four Worlds of the Kabbalah, and the great cathedrals of Europe embody

Below: The gods of ancient Egypt were often depicted in classic meditation postures.

the sacred geometry at the core of Greek philosophy. Even the material with which the Egyptians built their monuments had symbolic meaning. The four elements of fire, air, water and earth were represented by basalt, limestone, brick and sandstone.

What is not commonly known is that their pharaohs and gods were often depicted in poses which were the equivalent of the classic postures, or asanas, of yoga. In assuming these poses during meditation or ritual, an initiate of the Egyptian mysteries would be 'assuming the God form'. Each pose was thought to embody a specific aspect of the psyche, for each of the gods personified a human archetype. If, for example, you needed to draw upon higher

knowledge you could assume the form of Thoth, the scribe of the gods, and meditate on his attributes in the hope of receiving insights from what we would today call the higher self. These techniques were revived in the 19th century by the Hermetic Order of the Golden Dawn and found to be profoundly effective. They remain an integral part of the practices of many Western mystery schools to this day.

The Hermeticum

The practical and theoretical aspect of Egyptian mysticism and religion was preserved in a collection of Greek, Egyptian and Hebrew manuscripts known as the Corpus Hermeticum which is thought to have been compiled in the first and second centuries BC. The central theme of the work, which was attributed to a mythical figure, Hermes Trismegistos (the Greek name for the Egyptian god Thoth), was the unity of existence as revealed in the maxim, 'Whatever is below is like that which is above, and whatever is above is like that which is below'.

In one of the Greek tracts,

God is described as the light and the creation of the universe as the expression of His will. The means of manifestation we are told was sound, the uttering of 'a holy word', which was to be mythologized in the Christian concept of 'the Word'. The word is described in the Hermeticum as being 'the son of God' which implies that all living things were considered to be of divine origin and were galvanized by the divine spark:

'...for there is nothing that is not God. And do you say 'God is invisible?' Speak not so. 'Who is more manifest than God'.

The belief in the intrinsic power of certain sounds was a key element of Egyptian magic as it was to be in the mantras of Buddhism, the sacred names of God detailed in the Kabbalah and in the power of prayer in the Christian and Islamic traditions.

'Hermes saw the totality of things. Having seen, he understood, he had the power to reveal and show. And indeed, what he knew, he wrote down. What he wrote, he mostly hid away, keeping silence, rather than speaking out, so that every generation on coming into the world had to seek out these things.'

Main picture: Set, the god of night, the desert and of all evils; the symbol of the dark side of the psyche.

Esoteric orders and secret societies

Several modern esoteric orders and secret societies claim to be able to trace their origins back to the initiates of Ancient Egypt. Among these is AMORC (the Ancient and Mystical Order Rosae Crucis) which currently functions as an esoteric Open University of the New Age.

AMORC was founded in 1915 by American occultist H Spencer Lewis who wrote extensively on the subject of the mystical significance of the measurements of the pyramids and whose obsessional interest in Egypt found expression in the mock Egyptian structures which characterize the order's headquarters in California. The site today contains an Egyptian-style temple, a vast library, a planetarium, a museum of Egyptian artefacts and a university campus.

Students can attend courses in the Ageless Wisdom and psychic development either on campus in California or at a number of lodges in Europe. Alternatively, they can choose a course by correspondence which also covers related science subjects, plus philosophy, metaphysics, mysticism and parapsychology.

'As Brethren of the Rosy Cross, our personal endeavours, our minds, our laboratories, clinics and institutions are devoted to the rebuilding of the human race and the advancement of civilization.' (H Spencer Lewis)

The Rosicrucians

The Rosy Cross to which Lewis and his organization regularly refer is the Rosicrucian brotherhood, a quasi-mystical Christian secret society which sprang up spontaneously across Europe in the 17th century in response to the circulation of anonymous pamphlets calling for the establishment of a new order.

The pamphlets, which were almost certainly the creation of frustrated idealist and academic Johann Valentin von Andrea, purposely omitted to give an address to which interested individuals could respond. The result of this was that intellectuals and the esoterically inclined began to form their own lodges of the Rosy Cross embodying the principles outlined in the pamphlets. Past members of the fraternity are believed to have included: Goethe, Descartes, Leibniz, Sir Isaac Newton, Michael Faraday and Sir Francis Bacon.

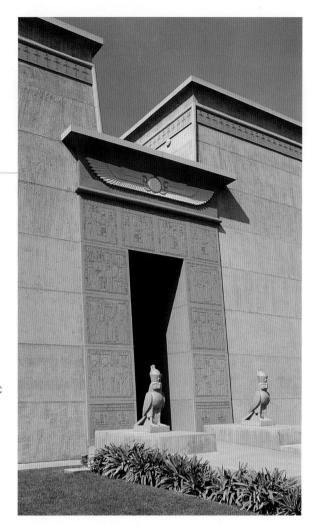

Right: The mock Egyptian facade of the AMORC administration building. Left: The symbol of the Rosicrucians, configurating the four elements.

Some of the Rosicrucian practices and concepts are thought to have been incorporated into the rituals and teachings of the Freemasons and later into the occult ceremonial rites of the Hermetic Order of the Golden Dawn.

Freemasonry

Modern freemasons can trace the origins of their philanthropic secret society to the establishment of the Grand Lodge in England in 1717, but the secret signs with which fellow members introduce themselves to each other are thought to date from the Middle Ages when itinerant stonemasons developed a method of establishing their level of skill to prospective employers. However, the order's elaborate initiation rituals are believed to date even further back, possibly to the building of Solomon's Temple in the 10th century BC, after which initiates incorporated the principles of cosmic proportion into the geometry of sacred buildings across Europe.

Every masonic temple incorporates Kabbalistic principles in its main features, specifically the two pillars of divine duality on either side of the main entrance, as they were in Solomon's temple. The chequered pattern of the floor of the central chamber symbolizes the interdependence of universal forces.

These occur again in the main teaching aid known as the Tracing Board, together with other symbols of duality which illustrate the idea that the same cosmic principles also operate on Earth. Among these are Jacob's Ladder which links heaven and earth, its three rungs symbolizing the three higher worlds of Emanation, Creation and Formation, although masons refer to these as Faith, Hope and Charity to express the attributes required of the members at each level or degree of initiation.

In their rituals too, the masons continue the analogy, with God described as being the Great Architect of the Universe. In the ritual of the Second Degree, for example, the generation of the second world in the ever unfolding fabric of existence (Beriah, the World of Creation) is described in technical terminology. The initiate is informed of the 'regular progression of science from a point to a line, from a line to a plane, from a plane to a solid'. In this analogy, he is made aware that every aspect of existence is an expression of the Will of the Great Architect who has manifested His Will through logical stages from conception of the idea to its embodiment in matter.

The Theosophical Society and the Golden Dawn

The course of what has been called the Ageless Wisdom has been likened to a golden thread running from ancient Egypt, through the esoteric teachings of the Judeo-Christian tradition, to be taken underground by a succession of heretical sects and secret societies, before finally emerging as an 'alternative world-view' in modern times.

So therefore, the 19th century can be seen as the time when the golden thread became entangled in the machinations of two distinctly different occult orders which were presided over by equally eccentric characters. However, despite the eccentric behaviour of their founders both The Hermetic Order of the Golden Dawn and the Theosophical Society continue to exert a profound influence on innumerable groups and individuals around the world. Several contemporary magical orders claim direct descent from the Golden Dawn and their methods of penetrating the unconscious are still widely practised today, while The Theosophical Society, whose motto remains: 'There is no religion higher than truth', survives as a source of spiritual philosophy more than a century after it was founded.

The Theosophical Society (1875-)

The principle aims of the Theosophical Society were the expression of the brotherhood of man regardless of race, creed, colour or social position; the study of comparative religion to establish a universal ethic and the development of the latent powers of the human soul.

The society's founding members were an unlikely couple of people. Colonel H S Olcott was a veteran of the American Civil War who had an obsessional interest in psychic phenomena and his larger-than-life partner, Helena Petrovna Blavatsky, was a Russian aristocrat who claimed mediumistic powers.

Olcott was evidently in awe of the charismatic HPB, as she became known, and rushed to her defence whenever her materializations and other 'marvellous phenomena' were questioned by sceptics, which was frequently the case. He was also a witness to her telepathic communications with what she referred to as her 'hidden masters', supreme spiritual beings who she claimed dictated the secrets of existence to her which she later published as Isis Unveiled (1877) and The Secret Doctrine (1891). Both books, which HPB described as the 'masterkey to the mysteries of ancient and modern science and theology', became bestsellers and were fundamental in introducing Victorian society to the concept of the supernatural. However, in retrospect they are undermined by a confusion of pseudo-Buddhist philosophy and a fanciful view of prehistory in which she traces the roots of the human race back to the mythical 'lost continent' of Atlantis.

Main picture: A youthful Aleister Crowley who was later to be dubbed 'the wickedest man in the world'.

The Hermetic Order of the Golden Dawn (1888–1900)

The Golden Dawn was an occult secret society which flourished in England at a time when there was intense interest in the supernatural among the cultured middle classes, although the order took pains to distance itself from the spurious world of spiritualism and psychic phenomena. Instead, they promoted themselves as the custodians of archaic wisdom, a policy which duly attracted an élite membership of artists, writers, intellectuals, mystics and 'freethinkers' including the poet W B Yeats, the writers Bram Stoker, Algernon Blackwood, Sax Rohmer and Arthur Machen and various members of the establishment.

Unfortunately, they also attracted the notorious magician Aleister Crowley whom the tabloid press had dubbed 'the wickedest man in the world' and for whom the promise of kabbalistic secrets and active participation in elaborate magical rituals had evidently proven irresistible. It was Crowley's vehement dislike of founder S L MacGregor Mathers, a man whom Yeats described as 'half lunatic, half knave', which eventually lead to the order's disintegration.

But for Yeats and the other genuinely curious minds membership promised revelatory insights into the workings of the unconscious mind and first-hand experience of the mysteries of life and death which the Rosicrucian brotherhoods and Masonic lodges had only theorized about.

Mathers claimed to have uncovered and translated ancient Graeco-Egyptian rituals which could summon the 'Divine Genius' or 'Higher Self' at will and also to have devised a system of symbols for penetrating the veil into the inner worlds (see pages 18–19).

The five so-called 'Knowledge Lectures', which served as the foundation of the order's initiation rites, included a discussion of the symbolic significance of the Hebrew Kabbalah. This was interwoven with elements of Egyptian and Enochian angel magic framed by Rosicrucian ritual to appease members from a Christian and masonic background.

Ironically, the acrimonious and widely publicized court battle between Crowley and Mathers which led to the final disintegration of the order also helped to disseminate these 'arcane secrets' to those who might make better use of them.

Left: Mercury as the Magus, from the tarot pack designed by Crowley.

Astral doorways

Among the many systems which the Hermetic Order of the Golden Dawn developed for enhancing psychic powers and exploring the invisible realms was that of the Tattwa symbols, a series of simple coloured shapes derived from the eastern esoteric tradition. The five major symbols consist of a yellow square, a blue circle, a red triangle, a silver horned moon on its back and a black or indigo oval representing the four elements of earth, air, fire and water plus the realm of spirit. By meditating upon these, either individually or in combination, it is claimed that you can gain instant access to other dimensions either through what Jung called 'active imagination' or by triggering an out-of-body-experience.

The procedure is a simple one which anyone can try for themselves.

Making your own Tattwa cards

To make your own Tattwa cards cut five white squares from cardboard to roughly the size of a standard playing card. The back of the cards should be left blank.

On the face of each card paint one of the five symbols (as illustrated) in strong, vivid colours and when they are dry either give them a coat of varnish or cover them with transparent artist's film.

Using the cards

There are two ways to use the cards. The first is simply to hold a card to your forehead, close your eyes and allow the images to arise spontaneously. In this respect the cards work in a strikingly similar way to the 'active imagination' exercises developed by Carl Jung. He was himself a student of esoteric techniques including using the I Ching and the practical, that is magical, Kabbalah.

In the second method lie flat on a bed or sit in a chair and relax your whole body so that you drift into a meditative state. When you feel sufficiently relaxed, stare at the chosen symbol for 30 seconds or so until its image has been imprinted on your retina. Then turn the card over and look at the blank side where the image will start to appear in a complementary colour.

Fix this image in your mind. Then close your eyes and internalize it into a glowing image as you would with the afterglow of a candle flame or a bright light.

Now, visualize the still glowing symbol being enlarged and when you lose sight of the edges, imagine yourself passing though it as if it was an actual entrance. When you have visualized this doorway behind you then you can begin to explore. Initially you will probably see either a symbol or a landscape on which symbols might spontaneously appear, the significance of which can be found in a reputable dictionary of symbols.

To return to waking consciousness simply become gradually aware of your body and your surroundings, counting down slowly from ten to one as you do so.

Messages for life

The cards were intended to explore the hidden depths of the unconscious and the invisible realms of the spirit at random, but you could formulate a specific question and trust to intuition to guide you to choose the relevant card. The symbol which you see may then have a relevance to your question.

Testing the Tattwa

After his first encounter with the cards the poet and mystic W B Yeats, himself an initiate of the Golden Dawn, was convinced that the symbols had a precise and objective meaning which could trigger access to the realms of the unconscious.

In his autobiography Yeats describes how S.L. MacGregor Mathers, a co-founder of the Golden Dawn, had persuaded him to hold one of these cards against his forehead and describe what he saw. He was then overwhelmed by an image he could not control. It was that of a black Titan rising from the ruins in a barren desert landscape which Mathers later explained was a Salamander or fire spirit. The card had evidently given access to one of the lower worlds inhabited by elemental spirits.

After this and similar experiences Yeats carried out several experiments of his own to test the effect of the symbols and to eliminate the possibility that the images were a creation of the imagination or influenced through telepathic contact between the participants. On one occasion he accidentally gave his subject the wrong symbol and the person 'saw' the scene appropriate to that symbol rather than the scene which Yeats was imagining. This suggests that the symbols are universal archetypes and not subjective. When Yeats visualized a symbol different to the one which his subject had been given then the imagery would be a composite of both elements.

It was Yeats conclusion that the images 'drew upon associations which are beyond the reach of the individual "subconscious"...that the borders of our memory are [ever] shifting, and that our memories are a part of one great memory, the memory of Nature herself, [and] that this...great memory can be evoked by symbols." It was an idea that anticipated Jung's concept of the Collective Unconscious by 30 years.

Kabbalah – The Tree of Life

On penetrating into the sanctuary of the Kabbalah one is seized with admiration in the presence of a doctrine so logical, so simple and at the same time so absolute...it establishes, by the counterpoise of two forces in apparent opposition, the eternal balance of being...', Eliphas Levi 'Transcendental Magic'

Kabbalah, the arcane Jewish metaphysical philosophy which forms the basis of the Western esoteric tradition, seeks to explain our place and purpose in existence through a symbolic diagram known as the Tree of Life.

In simple terms, the ten spheres, or sephiroth, which are arranged on the Tree and the 22 paths which connect them are symbolic of the divine attributes of the Creator and all that He created. By understanding and, to some extent, experiencing these qualities as they manifest themselves in us and our world (through the three disciplines of contemplation, devotion and action), practising Kabbalists aim to manifest their higher nature and attain union with the divine.

According to Kabbalistic tradition, the Universe came into being because God wished to know itself and express its love in the act of creation. To do so God the Immanent, the Absolute All (EN SOF), emerged from God the Transcendent, the Absolute Nothing (AYIN) in a gradual process of manifestation through realms of increasing density which are symbolized in the sephiroth.

Each sephirah, symbolizes the active Male and passive Female attributes of the

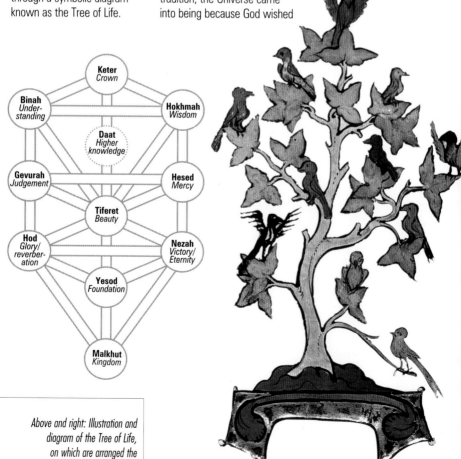

Above and right: Illustration and diagram of the Tree of Life, on which are arranged the Divine Attributes.

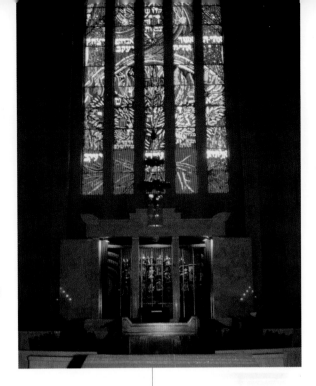

Creator and all that it created, although we are to remember that these are abstract concepts beyond human comprehension. However, for practical purposes we can consider the sephiroth as personifying the characteristics of a Heavenly Mother/Father figure, the Supreme Being (Keter), who is Wise (Hokhmah), Understanding (Binah), Merciful (Hesed), Just (Gevurah), Beautiful (Tiferet), Loving (Nezah), All-knowing (Hod) Perceptive (Yesod) and Discriminating (Malkuth).

Above: The Tree of Life depicted in stained glass in the Great Synagogue, Jerusalem.

Kabbalah philosophy

Kabbalah reveals that a world which appears to be in crisis and chaos is in fact simply in a state of becoming exactly what its creator intended. According to the tradition every element in the universe, including ourselves, is precisely in its right place in the cosmic scheme and continually evolving under the influence of the forces symbolized by the Tree. These complementary dynamics express themselves in the outer world as force and form, and within ourselves on one level as the male and female aspects of the personality. But as the principles of the Tree they resonate at every level – the physical, psychological and spiritual – these same attributes can be interpreted on the physical level as the active and passive functions of the body and on the etheric, or spiritual level, as expansion and contraction.

In crude terms the latter could be symbolized as good and evil, but in modern Kabbalah these are seen merely as the evolutionary impulse, as we aspire to the light and love of the divine, and the contrary inclination to remain in the darkness of ignorance for fear of change.

By becoming aware of the forces seeking expression in existence and the universal laws which govern these, we can begin to balance them and in the process develop greater self-awareness, a sense of purpose and an appreciation of the interdependence of all living things as a reflection of the source.

Contrary to popular myth no knowledge of Judaism or of the Hebrew language is necessary to work with the Kabbalah for it expresses a universal wisdom, albeit presented in a unique diagrammatic and philosophical form.

Learning from life

Unlike some of the Eastern disciplines it does not require practitioners to denounce their present religion, or lifestyle for an ascetic life in a spiritual commune. Kabbalah is a way of perceiving and learning from life, and does not offer an escape from our responsibilities. It abhors blind faith and instead requires all initiates to test the validity of its teachings for themselves within the give and take of human relationships and in the ferment of experience in the 'real world'. Otherwise the insights gained in meditation will have no lasting value or impact.

By working with the principles of the Kabbalah through the modern methods of pathworking and creative visualization initiates can safely experience the depths of their own psyche and the perfection of the higher realms. And having done so they can integrate those insights into their everyday experience to prove the value of the teachings for themselves.

Kabbalah envisages the descent of the Divine in terms of four distinct stages of creation. These are the worlds of Emanation (the realm of unity and perfection), Creation (of pure spirit), Formation (the astral realm) and Action (our physical world). We can all experience these for ourselves by raising our awareness from the physical world through the various psychological states to the spiritual dimension and ultimately, to the realm of pure spirit.

The method outlined below is a simple but potentially very powerful guided meditation known as 'rising in the chariot'. Although it has been stripped of its Hebrew allusions for practical purposes, it is otherwise presented in a form which has remained largely unchanged since biblical times.

Exercise:
The Cosmic Chariot

Begin by focusing on your breathing, establishing a four-two-four rhythm. That is counting up to four as you inhale, pausing at the top of the breath for a count of two, counting four as you exhale and pausing for another count of two before taking the next breath. As you do this become aware that this is the airy element in your physical body. Now focus on the blood circulating in your veins and maintaining the vital organs. Regard this as the watery element. Next become aware of the density of your body with the skeletal supporting structure and the flesh that gives you form. This is the earth element. Finally, focus on the heat in your skin which is the fire element and as you do so visualize this energy radiating outwards into your aura, saturating you in the vital force.

Now extend your awareness into the outer world. Go deep beneath your feet to the centre of the earth where the prima matter bubbles in pools of molten rock which will one day erupt in a

The Kabbalah teaches that all life is continually evolving and that the process of creation is never-ending.

stream of liquid fire to fashion new mountains.

Ascend through the multi-coloured layers of rock, minerals and crystals to the surface where the waters of the world ebb and flow under the influence of the moon, where waves lap upon the shoreline and where, inland, mountain streams form forest pools and vast lakes.

Now feel a fresh breeze upon your face and listen to the rustle of leaves as the wind gathers strength buffeting rain clouds across the sky.

Rise up and follow the clouds, sail with them through the vast starlit ocean of the sky. Look back upon the earth turning below and sense the earth infusing the energy of the sun as do all forms of life upon the planet.

Now that you have experienced the fire, water, air and earth elements in the physical realm it is time to ascend to the realm of spirit.

Rise up into the blackness of space towards a spiral of stars in the far distance. As you approach you will see that it is not a cluster of stars, but a spiral of luminous celestial beings, a tunnel of light. You are drawn into this tunnel of light by an irresistible sense of love and belonging.

Enter the celestial kingdom, the realm of the archangels and evolved souls who serve the creator, and abide in their company until you feel the urge to return.

This is Beriah, the world of Creation, the realm of essence where form and force are brought into balance to bring order from chaos. Here dwell the evolved souls who have broken free of the wheel of life, death and rebirth, but who chose to continue to influence the spiritual progress of human kind from the world of spirit or by descent into the flesh. Here exists the Bodhisattvas of the Buddhist tradition, the Avatars worshipped by the Hindu and the Messianic figures of the Judeao-Christian tradition.

When you are ready begin the descent back to earth. Leave the angelic realm and drift down through the spiral of light into the dimension of time and space. Be drawn to our solar system, linger briefly over the Earth and then descend through the clouds. Sail over the seas, see the coastline approaching and follow the road that leads you home. Become aware once again of your surroundings, the density of your body, your breath and when you are ready return to waking consciousness.

Reincarnation

It is estimated that over half of the world's population believe in reincarnation; the idea that we are all reborn many times over. The fact that we cannot recall our previous lives is explained as being a fail-safe mechanism to avoid complications in this life and to allow us to make a fresh start. However, researchers have uncovered a considerable number of cases where memories of past lives have been reawakened spontaneously and of others which have been stirred to the surface of consciousness by a comparatively new technique known as regression therapy.

It is thought that the increasing interest in reincarnation in the West signifies our gradual acceptance of a greater reality and marks the beginning in the next stage of our evolution. The implications of ultimately proving reincarnation to be a fact of life are considerable. But even simply accepting the possibility can have a considerable effect on how we live our current lives, perhaps reducing the intensity and stress that we put ourselves under in the belief that we have to fit everything into one brief lifetime.

Past lives

Prior to the 1950s, reincarnation was an alien idea to Westerners who, if they were aware of it at all, would

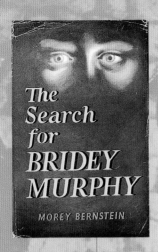

The
Search
for
BRIDEY
MURPHY

MOREY BERNSTEIN

*Above and main picture:
The case of Colorado housewife
Virginia Tighe introduced the
concept of reincarnation to
the West.*

have regarded it as a concept exclusive to the Hindu tradition. Then in the early 1950s the case of a Colorado housewife, Virginia Tighe, became the subject of an international bestseller. The Search For Bride Murphy by psychoanalyst Morey Bernstein recorded his patient's detailed recollections of a past life as an Irishwoman during the first half of the 19th century. Mrs Tighe is said to have recalled the names of shops in County Cork and to have described antiquated farming methods. She even entertained her analyst with popular songs of the period and the minutiae of rural life in the language of the time and in the dialect peculiar to the district. Her information subsequently proved to be correct.

A movie was made based on the book and public fascination with the case appeared to have reached a peak when it was revealed that Mrs Tighe had an Irish nurse during her own childhood. It was assumed that the nurse

had been the source of the information and the public lost interest. But even if Mrs Tighe had merely been recalling details that her nurse had once told her there are too many aspects of the case which could not be so conveniently explained.

Less well known, but even more convincing, was the case of Shanti Devi, a young Indian girl whose past life recollections became the subject of intense scrutiny and exhaustive research by Professor Ian Stevenson of the University of Virginia School of Medicine in the USA and the Indian government.

In 1929 three-year old Shanti began regaling her parents with stories about her life with her husband and children, but they dismissed these as a childhood fantasy. By the time she was seven Shanti had sketched in her stories with considerable detail including the names and descriptions of her family, the name of the town, Muttra, and the fact that she had died in 1925 giving birth to a fourth child. She claimed that her name had been Ludgi and her husband was called Kedarnath.

Although the town she named did in fact exist, Shanti's parents were concerned for her sanity and consulted a doctor. He was stunned to hear her describe medical procedures that a child could not possibly have known.

Then fate took a hand. An acquaintance of Shanti's father called unannounced and she immediately greeted him as her husband's cousin. The man confirmed that he lived in Muttra and that he did in fact have a cousin called Kedarnath whose wife Ludgi had died in childbirth.

A former husband

Her parents then arranged for Kedarnath to call without informing their daughter, but she recognized and identified him immediately. Inevitably, perhaps, she then became the subject of a rigorous scientific investigation and was taken to Muttra for the first time by government researchers whom she led through the town while blindfolded. When they removed the blindfold she was able to take them straight to Ludgi's house. There she was reunited with her children as well as her husband's parents and brother, all of whom she correctly identified. The only person she failed to recognize was the fourth child that she had died giving birth to.

On a subsequent visit to Muttra, to see the house of Ludgi's mother, Shanti noted the changes that had been made to the Ludgi's house since her death and led the investigators to a place where Ludgi had hidden her rings. Not even her husband had known that they were buried there.

Karma

The Buddha said 'what you are is what you have done, what you will be is what you do now'.

Central to the belief in reincarnation is the concept of karma, one of the most misunderstood aspects of the Eastern spiritual tradition and one which has significance for seekers of all persuasions. This is because it explains why things are the way they are, how we each created the characteristics that we possess, what drives us to make certain decisions, and why we inherited our present circumstances.

Although it is commonly believed that both karma and reincarnation were exclusively Eastern ideas, both were in fact fundamental to Jewish mysticism and in turn to early Christianity. Jesus, who is believed to have been an initiate of the Jewish mystical sect known as the Essenes, expressed the belief in the phrase: 'As you sow so shall you reap', but in 553 AD the Church decreed both concepts to be a heresy.

Contrary to popular belief, Karma (which translates as 'action') is not to be confused with predestination or fate. There is no supernatural agency involved and no element of judgement and punishment for 'past sins'. Karma is not a burden placed upon us, but a dynamic whose effect is determined by our response to experiences. The law of karma states that the experiences we attract are dictated by our past actions, thoughts and desires and it is our reaction to these experiences that are more significant than the experiences themselves. So it is as important to take responsibility for our reactions as it is for our actions.

If we treat each experience as part of a learning process then our 'karmic burden' will be

Right: The Buddhist Wheel of Life.

Above: A yogi buries his head in the sand, stops breathing and reduces his pulse rate to demonstrate mind over matter.

diminished and the experiences themselves will contribute towards our inner growth and greater awareness. We are to see difficulties as a completion of a process that we ourselves have brought into being, usually unconsciously, in order to force us to face the purpose for which we are on earth. If we accept this, then we can no longer indulge in useless regrets or blame ourselves for making mistakes as it was the mistake that has brought us to the truth of a situation.

Cause and effect

Karma is no more than the natural law of cause and effect which states that our actions, speech and even our thoughts bring a corresponding result. Seen in this light, karma is neither 'good' nor 'bad' but neutral and can be accumulated and cleared in this present lifetime.

The consequences of our actions or failure to act, do not always bring instant results, just as failing to repair a faulty tap may not bring disaster until we've turned it once too often. And so it is with karma which has a cumulative effect, the results of which are often delayed, sometimes into later lifetimes.

Karma is continually unfolding in subtle ways, but to take an extreme example, a murderer might choose to reincarnate in circumstances in which he or she has the opportunity to make amends to their victim. Karma does not

mean that they would become a victim themselves as that would only place a burden on their murderer and so the cycle of violence would continue eternally. But a murderer would also have the free will to make the same 'mistake' over and over again, to commit the same type of crime, and it is this karmic struggle between our destructive and evolutionary impulses which we express in crude terms as being 'good' and 'evil'.

The Tibetan Buddhist masters taught that the imprints of our past actions are stored like seeds in what we in the West would call the unconscious. When similar conditions arise again these imprints 'germinate' and manifest as circumstances and situations in our lives. In this way we reinforce our habitual tendencies and this determines the course of our life, our state of mind at the moment of our death, and the circumstances of our next incarnation.

There is a Tibetan saying: 'If you want to know your past life, look into your present condition; if you want to know your future life, look at your present actions.'

Karmic belief

It is taught that the law of karma is infallible and inevitable, that whenever we harm other people we are accumulating a debt that must one day be repaid. But conversely, whenever we help or bring happiness to others we are ensuring our own future happiness.

Neither God nor karma dictates the course and quality of our lives, we do. All that we are and all that we have brought into being is the direct consequence of our past thoughts and actions, not the blessings of a benevolent creator. That is why it is self-defeating to attribute every 'blessing' to providence, because that implies that we fear it could also be taken away. Fear, is also the real disease that creates all our problems. Karma does not contradict the concept of free will; in fact it is the ultimate expression of our divine nature.

Yoga

Yoga is the art of using your mind to control your body and thereby achieving self-discipline in its truest sense.

In the East it has been developed as a rather extreme ascetic discipline to illustrate the spirit's mastery of the body and to demonstrate almost superhuman feats of endurance. But in its more popular Western form it uses simple relaxation exercises, postures, meditation techniques and mantras to increase physical energy, improve health and create peace of mind.

The eight limbs of yoga

Yoga was developed in the East 4,000 years before the birth of Christianity as a means of controlling physical desire, which it was thought was responsible for chaining the soul to the wheel of rebirth. Yoga was considered a secret discipline to be taught only to those who had 'pacified' their lower natures and who were intent on ultimately attaining Samadhi, perfect union with God.

To achieve this blissful state the yogi initiates were required to follow the eight limbs of yoga which included adherence to a moral code known as the five restraints (yama) and the mastering of five disciplines (niyama). Yama instils the importance of truthfulness, honesty, moderation, non-possessiveness and non-violence, while niyama teaches purity, contentment, study of the sacred texts, austerity and a constant awareness of the divine. In addition to these the yogi must practise asana (the postures), pranayama (breath control), pratyahara (emptying of the mind), dharana (concentration) dhayana (disassociation with the physical body) and sustaining the state of samadhi (superconsciousness).

Of these a person starting yoga should initially concentrate on pranayama (breath control) which in the early stages involves establishing a regular and natural rhythm to still the mind and regulate the flow of energy around the etheric and physical body. If necessary, you can use a count of four-two-four-two to establish a steady rhythm, that is a count of four with each breath taken in, holding the breath for a count of two, then exhaling for four and pausing at the bottom of the breath for another count of two.

The ten paths of yoga

It is a popular misconception that yoga is solely concerned with the practice of the physical postures. The asanas, of which there are more than 1,000, are only one aspect of what are known as the ten paths of yoga. Hatha yoga is the form of yoga that teaches the asanas, or postures, which were developed to achieve mastery over the body so that its needs did not interfere with prolonged meditation.

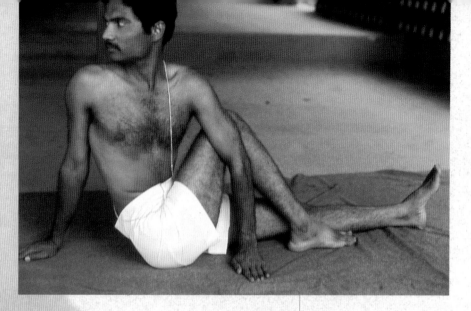

Above: The Vakra asana, one of more than 1000 yogic postures.

Other types of yoga relate to different areas:

Bhakti yoga concentrates on praise and devotion to Brahman (God).

Dhyana yoga focuses on meditation and contemplation.

Juana yoga involves the study of the Hindu sacred texts known as the Vedata in pursuit of wisdom.

Karma yoga is the way of action through charitable deeds and devotion to the needs of others.

Kriya yoga involves religious observance and attention to the details of ritual.

Kundalini yoga is an advanced form of meditation which aims to awaken the 'sleeping serpent' of evolutionary energy coiled in the base chakra. Those who have tapped this powerful source describe an overpowering force surging up from the base of the spine to

strike the brain like a stream of liquid light. It is thought that this energy will seep into our chakras as our awareness increases and we evolve spiritually, but to stimulate the release of kundalini without the supervision of an experienced meditation teacher can have a traumatic effect on the psyche.

Laya yoga is concerned with energizing and centring the chakras through the chanting of mantras.

Mantra yoga uses chants to harmonize the etheric energy centres and lines within the body and to raise mental awareness by tuning the mind to a higher 'frequency'. A mantra can be a single significant word or phrase which is repeated out loud

during meditation to help focus attention, block intrusive thoughts and set up a sympathetic vibration within the body. Two of the most common mantras are AUM (thought to be the sound of Creation itself) and AUM-MANI-PADME-HUM.

Raja yoga has been called the 'royal road' because it focuses on knowledge of Brahman and the world of spirit.

Each of these paths have been taught as if they were the expressions of different traditions, but they are in essence complementary and all aim to guide the practitioner to the same state of bliss and self-awareness.

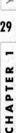

Five of the basic yoga postures as outlined below can be practised unsupervised by the beginner in combination with breath control and mantras, or they can be practised as a purely physical exercise.

● *The Dragon* – kneel on the floor on a padded surface with your buttocks resting on your heels, and your toes turned under. Place your palms on your thighs, keep your head erect and back upright. Breathe in a relaxed and natural rhythm and hold the posture for 30 seconds.

● *The God* – make yourself comfortable sitting in a straight backed chair with your head erect, knees together, palms on thighs and eyes closed. Breathe in a relaxed and natural rhythm and hold the posture for 30 seconds.

● *The Ibis* – from a standing position bend your left leg behind you to take your left ankle in your right hand and stand as steady as possible. As

Left: one of the most basic yoga postures; the Ibis.

you do so, place the forefinger of your left hand to your lips. Breathe in a relaxed and natural rhythm and hold the posture for 30 seconds. On a subsequent session practise taking the right ankle in the left hand.

● *The Lotus* – the classic sitting and meditation pose. Sit cross-legged with your heels resting on the back of the opposite thighs, with your palms resting just above your knees with your forefinger and thumb together.

● *The Maricyasana* – a simple yogic twist used for relieving tension in the shoulders and neck and to increase mobility in the spine. Sit on the floor and double back your left leg so that it lays next to your right buttock. Place your right leg over your left leg to form a triangle with the floor, with your right foot flat on the floor. Rest the left palm on the right foot and twist

gently to face away, with the side of your chest side touching your right thigh.

Once you are able to regulate your breathing for ten minutes without fidgeting or altering your posture you can attempt to incorporate pratyahara into your routine by using the basic meditation techniques as described on pages 144 and 146. Pratyahara is the ability to empty the mind of all thoughts by concentrating on nothingness.

If after a month you feel that you are progressing well you can move on to the next stage, which is the use of a mantra to help in focusing your attention.

The following month you could intensify your practice by increasing your total daily exercise time from an initial 10-minute routine to 20 minutes and attempt the more difficult postures.

If you have managed to attain the state of pratyahara for ten minutes without having to make a great effort then move on to develop dharana. This is the ability to concentrate on a single thought, simple object or a point either in front of you or in your mind's eye. The most practical exercise of this kind is

to focus on a point in the mind's eye for the first week, imagining it as a pinpoint of light or a white dot on a blackboard, and developing this into a line during the second week and then as a cross the week after. From there it is possible to 'draw' a simple mandala or sacred symbol before moving on to more elaborate visualization exercises for self-healing, protection from negativity, or to attract whatever you want into your life.

Mastering these disciplines eventually leads to dhyana in which the object of meditation is the self, the person who is meditating. Visualizing yourself with detachment in this way helps to develop a disassociation with your physical body, leading to the disintegration of the ego and the manifestation of the higher self from your unconscious.

Shamanism

In 1959 an American anthropologist, Professor Michael Harner, travelled to the Peruvian Amazon to live with the Conibo Indians and learn the mysteries of shamanism at first hand. Shamanism is probably the earliest form of spiritual exploration to have been practised by primitive man and in many remote regions of the world from Alaska to Australia it survives as the spiritual expression of indigenous peoples. It is a visionary tradition based on an animistic world-view which holds that nature is alive with spirits and deities with whom the shaman can communicate and draw upon as a source of wisdom, healing, divination and magic. A number of techniques are used to induce the trance states that allow the shaman's soul to enter the spirit realm including dancing, chanting, rhythmic drumming, fasting, vision quests (a form of meditation similar to creative visualization) and the ingestion of natural hallucinogenics.

Professor Harner was persuaded by the Conibo to ingest the juice of the 'soul vine' ayahuasca in order to experience the spirit world for himself and was duly confronted by images of dragon-headed soul boats, a giant crocodile and humans with bird's heads. He dismissed the experience as subjective, a stream of consciousness similar to a bad drug 'trip' or nightmare, but was later astonished to meet an Amazonian shaman who described precisely the same creatures and landscape from his own experience.

Urban shamans

Professor Harner subsequently became one of the world's leading authorities on shamanism, writing a number of bestselling books on the subject and holding workshops which showed how these ancient techniques could be adapted to modern needs. This interest in turn led to the appearance of a new generation of urban shaman in Europe and the USA who now practise the healing arts as an 'alternative therapy'.

Although westerners have tended to see shamanism as a superstitious remnant of our pagan past there is evidence that its practices can stimulate a profound spiritual experience. An Altaian shaman, for example, will cut notches in a birch tree before venturing forth in spirit so that the villagers can follow his progress as he describes his ascent through the various heavens. This belief in their being several strata of the spirit world has striking similarities to the 'seven heavens' of Sumerian and Semitic belief from which we derive the phrase 'to be in seventh heaven'.

Saul of Tarsus (later St Paul), who is believed to have been a practising Kabbalist, described 'ascending in the spirit' through the heavens to achieve direct knowledge of the Mysteries and numerous mystics throughout history have described similar journeys through various dimensions that have subsequently been mythologized as Heaven and Hell.

One Eskimo shaman has described the sensations he felt after enduring a painful

Main picture: The Nazca lines etched into the Peruvian desert are thought to have been central to shamanic ceremonies.

Above: Shamanic figure depicting the tribal shaman in meditation.

physical ordeal designed to separate the mind from the body in terms which invite comparison with the mystical experience: 'I could see and hear in a totally different way. I had gained my enlightenment, the shaman's light of brain and body, and this in such a manner that it was not only I who could see through the darkness of life, but the same bright light also shone out of me, imperceptible to human beings, but visible to all spirits of earth and sky and sea, and these now came to me as my helping spirits.'

Shamanic ceremonies

These were designed to lure animals to a chosen spot where they could be hunted and killed for food, but animals could also be called upon to be messengers from the spirit world.

In the 1970s a British explorer, Ross Salmon, was allowed to film a shamanistic ceremony of the Callawaya Indians of northern Bolivia in which a sacred condor bird was called upon to 'judge' a girl accused of infidelity. The condor is a notoriously shy bird which is rarely seen in the vicinity of human beings, but within 30 minutes of being summoned by three shaman priests a large male condor accompanied by two females flew directly overhead before landing within a few feet of the accused girl. While Salmon's cameraman kept the bird in shot the male condor ran towards the girl and put its beak to her throat. But before it could strike a member of the film crew threw a stone which frightened it off. A few days later the girl committed suicide convinced that the spirits had judged her guilty.

Paganism

Shortly after the Second World War Professor Geoffrey Webb, then Secretary of the Royal Commission on Historical Monuments, made a startling discovery whilst assessing bomb damage in an old country church. Hidden inside the altar, before which generations of orthodox Christians had worshipped in the name of Christ, was a stone phallus. Further investigation led to the discovery of similar carvings in 90 per cent of all churches built in Britain before the 14th century. But it was not the only curious feature that these old country churches had in common. Many had carvings of naked squatting female figures known as Sheila-na-gigs which were to be found in plain view of the congregation. It seems likely that these were symbolic representations of the mother goddess worshipped by the pagans. Neither of these features are to be found in churches built after 1350, when the persecution of witches became widespread in the wake of the Black Death, which suggests that the plague may have been the single shock that finally severed the population's attachment to a nameless fertility cult predating the Druids.

Pagan sites

It appears that almost all of the old churches had been erected on sites sacred to the pagans, not to erase 'the old religion' as was previously thought, but in an effort to appease the old gods and the local people who still worshipped them. Even pagan festivals were incorporated into the Church calendar. But after the plague (1348) the old gods were demonised; the horned nature god Pan became the Devil, Lucifer, the consort of the moon goddess was no longer the light-bringer but a fallen angel and paganism was corrupted in the popular imagination as witchcraft, the vilest of heresies.

The truth of our pagan past is believed to be found in the monuments scattered across the landscape of Europe and in the rites and rituals practised there, not in the lurid horror fiction of modern times nor in the hysterical fantasies which formed the basis of the prosecution in the witch trials.

In The Silbury Treasure – The Great Goddess Rediscovered, author Michael Dames, a senior lecturer at Birmingham Polytechnic, argues that the huge prehistoric mound known as Silbury Hill and its unusually shaped moat is a pregnant sheila-na-gig seen in profile. He relates that every August 7th (Lammas Eve), when the corn was ripe for cutting, the local inhabitants would gather beneath the summit to watch the earth mother giving birth helped by the moon goddess. From this vantage point the moon appears like a child's head from between the squatting mother's legs. It moves up the mound coming to rest on the belly then moves up to the breast where it appears to be feeding while its reflection in the water of the moat mimics flowing milk.

Stonehenge may have served a similar purpose, with its inner circle of stones representing the womb, which would have been symbolically penetrated by the phallic shadow cast by the rising moon over the Heel Stone.

Neopaganism

Although it is not possible to know for certain the details of pagan beliefs and practices in ancient times, it is thought that they share certain principles with the neopagan movement that is currently enjoying a revival. It is estimated that there are 100,000 practising pagans in the USA, for example, many of whom class themselves as wiccans, a term derived from the old English word 'wicce' meaning 'witch' (see pages 36–37). Neopagans revere nature which they believe is animated by spirits and that nature in all its diversity is an expression of the deity which is all pervading and multifarious. They also subscribe to a belief in reincarnation and practise ceremonial magic. The British anthropologist Tanya Luhrmann has interviewed many witches and discovered the attraction to be a 'need to be childlike, to marvel at nature and to re-experience an imaginative intensity that they had lost.'

The writer and witch known only as 'Starhawk' makes the distinction between wicca and orthodox religion by observing that wicca rejects dogma, scriptures and sacred literature of any kind. It doesn't venerate past masters nor consider them as being spiritually superior to other human beings, but takes its 'teachings from nature and reads inspiration in the movements of the sun, moon and stars, in the flight of birds, in the slow growth of trees and in the cycles of the seasons.'

Left: A Druid ceremony at Stonehenge, invoking the Mother Goddess.

Wicca

Contrary to popular belief Witchcraft, or Wicca as it is now called, has nothing to do with malevolent witches worshipping the devil, riding on broomsticks or casting curses. Neither do its current practitioners indulge in wild orgies as is sometimes reported. Such lurid images are largely the creation of the early Church who saw 'the Old Religion' as a potential threat to its authority and to its hold over an uneducated community.

Now, with the decline in orthodox religion and the increasing interest in alternative beliefs, Wicca has revived and is becoming more popular, particularly among young women who see it as a natural expression of their feminine spirituality.

The Craft, as it is also called, has cast off its image as a fringe cult to become the fastest growing alternative religion in America where it is estimated that there are now over half a million practitioners. Whatever its past, it has now successfully re-styled itself as a benign form of folk magic based on the worship of nature and the celebration of each individual's affinity with the forces of creation.

Wiccans do not appeal to, or acknowledge, the existence of external discarnate beings, only the all pervading life force, and so there is no supernatural element to their practises.

What Wiccans believe

There is no orthodoxy in Wicca, but all branches share the belief that there is a unity to existence and that every living thing has a sacred spirit whose power can be drawn upon for various purposes. These purposes are defined by their code of conduct which has been variously expressed as 'Love, and do harm to none', 'Perfect love, perfect trust' and 'Love, and do what you will under the law of love'.

The people who honour these principles are considered to be good witches and those who seek self-gratification or dominance over others are condemned by the majority of practitioners as being corrupt. The concept of there being black and white witches is a

Below: A modern male witch uses an altar as a visual focus of worship.

popular fallacy, in the same way as there are no wholly good or evil people.

Celebrating the seasons

Although it is primarily a feminine form of worship, there are a substantial number of male followers who are also known as witches. The presence of male and female energies are seen as vital in their ceremonies which celebrate fertility and the seasons at the vernal and autumnal equinoxes and also on the summer and winter solstices.

At such times the High Priestess who presides over each coven is considered as a personification of the Mother Goddess. The High Priest is seen as her consort, the Horned God, a Pan-like figure whom the early Church corrupted into the devil.

In these ceremonies, or

sabbats to use the traditional term, a circle will be drawn and consecrated with a saline solution. A candle will be placed at each of the four cardinal points, and at each one the High Priestess will evoke the four elements of fire, air, water and earth. If a fertility rite is to be performed this will usually be a symbolic union between the High Priestess and the High Priest who will use a consecrated dagger known as an athame and a chalice to represent the male and female elements.

People who find such ceremonies too theatrical, or who are unable or unwilling, to join a coven can work alone using modern variations on the arcane techniques such as candle magic, healing, banishings, blessings and talismanic magic.

Spells

Casting spells is still a central skill of the witches' art, but these now take a form that is almost indistinguishable from other forms of visualization exercises. The following bond-breaking spell is a typical example:

'To free oneself of an emotional attachment it is important to act out of compassion for both of the "enslaved" souls and not to

Above: A Wicca initiation ceremony performed within a protecting circle of salt.

cast the spell out of self-interest.

Cast a circle around yourself either in your mind or with chalk to focus your mental energy and to impress upon the unconscious the unity of all beings.

Begin with an invocation to the Mother Goddess in words of your own choosing asking for assistance in loosening the bonds and releasing both parties with a blessing that they may find what is right for them. This should be said three times.

Now visualize the other person with strands running from the key centres of their body to yours and imagine them breaking as you say:

"Head to head we break the thread we are free and we are blessed".

Repeat the verse, substituting the names of each of the vital energy centres (the throat, heart, solar plexus, sacral centre and base) as you envisage the bonds breaking. Finally, see the other person surrounded in light and wish them well on their journey through life'.

Natural and modern magic

Difficult though it may be to believe, in this digital age an increasing number of people are claiming that the path to personal transformation is to be found through the practice of ritual magic. In seeking to exorcise the demons and dogma of the Dark Ages and to distance themselves from the enduring image of the magus as one who indulges in forbidden rites, unintelligible incantations and the invocation of spirits and demons, the modern initiate draws parallels between the principles of practical magic and modern psychology.

In the spiritual supermarket that we call the New Age movement, magic is now promoted as a unified system of self-discovery and personal development. The source of true magic, we are told, is within us all.

As long ago as 1938 Israel Regardie, a former member of the Hermetic Order of the Golden Dawn and secretary to the notorious Aleister Crowley, described analytical psychology and ritual magic as two complementary aspects of a single system whose ultimate aim is the integration of the human personality. He compared them to the mind and body which he envisaged as being dual manifestations of an interior dynamic which some might call the soul or the Higher Self.

It is this essence of our being that the magician addresses when he or she impresses their will upon the unconscious during a magical ritual, just as one does when practising creative visualization or repeating affirmations in an effort to stop smoking or increase self-confidence.

Speaking to the unconscious

The practice of ritual magic is no more than the act of communicating with the unconscious in the belief that it will act to bring about what we desire. How it does this is unknown, but it is possible that the unconscious makes an impression upon the Universal Mind, the Collective Unconscious and that this pattern or matrix of mental energy filters down through the spiritual, mental and astral realms to manifest in the physical dimension in the desired form just as iron filings form a pattern around the invisible energy field surrounding a magnet.

Magic in its truest sense is at the core of every creative act, every idea that we bring into physical manifestation, from conceiving children to planning our home and it is the mechanism by which we draw upon our latent strengths whenever we 'psych ourselves up' to perform extraordinary feats. Magic is a natural ability

that we all possess because we all have the imagination to envisage whatever we desire and we also have the mental energy to bring that inner vision to life. However, most of us do not attract that which we secretly desire or wish for because we have not yet learnt how to focus our latent mental powers.

Links with meditation

This technique by which we can still our busy minds is still seen by the average person as slightly eccentric, while magic is widely regarded as being either silly, superstitious or even satanic. However, magic is neither 'good' nor 'evil'. It is the intention behind the desire that determines whether one is working with or against the universal laws. Neither is magic an easy option promising something for nothing. Like any other demanding spiritual discipline you only get out of it what you are prepared to put in.

Magic is just one step removed from meditation in that it seeks to impress a specific and clearly defined aim upon the unconscious using elaborate preparations and theatrical rituals. The magical act or ritual is purely symbolic; the invocations, symbols and stagecraft have no inherent power of their own; it is the inner, psychological work that produces the results. In this respect magic is no different from a religious rite in that both are designed to raise the level of consciousness from the mundane to the spiritual, but are effective only if performed in the right spirit.

A magical rite

The American magician, lecturer and author Nancy Watson cites her first experience of magic at the age of 15 as a good example of how magic can manifest in the material world. In December 1961 Nancy was working as a professional actress in a small production and had developed a crush on an older male member of the cast. When the play closed she was afraid that she would not see him again and so decided to work a

simple rite that would ensure she would meet him on a specific date in the near future. She chose 1pm on February 24, 1962.

Some weeks later she was invited to a theatrical gathering on February 24. As she walked into the theatre Nancy noticed the time, 12:59, and a moment later was greeted enthusiastically by the man who incorrectly addressed her as 'Judy'. The ritual had worked but she had forgotten to specify that he should recognize her when he saw her! The next time she saw him was on February 24 the following year and again a year later on February 24, 1964, after which her romantic fascination with him had faded and the bond was broken. After that, she never saw him again.

Above: The practise of modern magic is in marked contrast to the lurid images in horror fiction and films.
Main picture: Artist and magician Austin Osman Spare claimed to find inspiration for his paintings on the astral plane.

CHAPTER 2

TUNING IN TO MOTHER EARTH

In the late 1960s when geologist James Loveock introduced the idea that the Earth may be a living being he was hailed by ecologists and derided by the scientific establishment. Since then the concept has begun to permeate the popular consciousness and raised awareness of the consequences to be suffered from the slow poisoning of our planet. The melting of the polar ice caps, the depletion of the ozone layer and the extreme weather conditions that we have experienced as a result of the greenhouse effect are certainly signs for concern. However, there also appear to be equally powerful forces, within the Earth and in the life forms that it sustains (some of which are discussed here) which can have a subtle but significant influence on human behaviour and health of which many of us are unaware.

The Logan Stone, Bodmin Moor, England. Our ancestors raised monuments and buried mounds at sacred sites where the earth energy was strongest.

The nature of the universe

Science is finally beginning to acknowledge what the mystics have known for millennia; that our physical world of form is an illusion. There is no such thing as solid matter, everything is energy, matter is simply energy in another state, moving at a slower vibrational rate to give the illusion of form.

In the same way that our brain can be fooled into thinking that the images on a cinema screen are moving when they are really no more than a continuous ribbon of still frames, so our senses are continually filtering out whatever exists at the higher vibrational frequencies to give the illusion that we are living in 'the real world'. It is no wonder that many people dismiss momentary glimpses of these other realities as figments of their imagination. Psychic abilities such as clairvoyance and psychometry are simply an increased sensitivity to these other dimensions caused by a momentary glitch in our 'filter' or 'censoring' system. The 'censor' is necessary because without it we would be unable to distinguish between what is real (that is, what exists in the physical world) and what is immaterial (that is, of spirit). Unfortunately, the censor works a little too well and the lack of any kind of psychic insight can cultivate a blinkered view in which the physical world and its transient pleasures are greatly over-valued.

Universal laws

However, the world of science and the world of the spirit are gradually being seen not as contradictory but as complementary, the laws of physics and the universal laws being one and the same. The first universal law to which science is slowly coming to terms is encapsulated in the ancient maxim 'As above, so below', which conveys the fact that our physical world is the densest manifestation of this energy, but that other realities which mirror our own may exist in the spaces in between. Science acknowledges that existence is a spectrum of energy and that particles known as neutrinos, one of the four basic building blocks of life, are so small that they can pass through 'solid' matter. At present our perception of these worlds appears to be limited by the range of our organs and our fail-safe 'censor'.

The second universal law states that each human is a microcosm, a universe in miniature and that to understand the mysteries of existence we first have to understand ourselves, our true nature. It is no coincidence that the evolution of the universe can be compared to the life cycle of a human being. In the beginning, before the big bang, approximately 5 thousand million years ago, there was only pure energy. This oneness can be likened to a unfertilized human ovum, a single cell in which all the elements of life

Above: Every atom in existence originated in the Big Bang, 10–20 billion years ago.

and its potential are present but which remains unrealized until it can manifest, grow and begin to understand itself through experience.

All that had been manifested in existence before the big bang was at that moment compressed into a 'cell' the size of a garden pea and millions of times hotter than the centre of the sun. With the Big Bang this energy exploded into empty space as particles; photons (which we

perceive as light), neutrinos (so small that they pass through 'solid' matter), electrons (negatively charged particles) and positrons (positively charged electrons). As these condensed they formed atoms which became the building blocks of matter. Since then the universe has been moving inexorably towards higher states of order and greater complexity of form, just as we do in maturing from an infant to an adult. The impulse behind this evolutionary process is an ever increasing spiral of exchange between the life force and consciousness.

In our physical body and in our psyche we contain all the stages that the life force has passed through in the process which culminated with our creation. As we evolve and experience living our understanding filters back down to the 'lower' forms of life which in turn are raised in consciousness for everything is energy and so everything is 'alive' in a sense.

God is everything

The inevitable conclusion to which this alternative world-view leads us is to the idea that what we call God is not a separate entity sitting in judgement on us somewhere 'out there', but is everything that is manifest and unmanifest in existence. Everything is God. And if God is all, then evil cannot exist as a separate conscious entity either, because anything that is perfect cannot create anything that is imperfect. Evil must be manufactured. It must be our deliberate acts of inhumanity which deny our true divine nature, the contrary impulse which tends to contraction rather than expansion, stagnation rather than growth. To act in harmony with the evolutionary impulse and realize our true nature we must first work on ourselves and through our influence hope to raise the consciousness and awareness of those with whom we come into contact. Only in that process can we hope to bring a New Age into being.

Standing stones

In 1934 a Scottish engineer, Alexander Thom, was idly admiring a megalithic stone circle that stood on a hilltop overlooking Loch Roag in the Outer Hebrides when it occurred to him that the avenue of menhirs were in perfect alignment with the pole star. However, in the 5th millennium BC the celestial map would have looked very different and so the stones could not have been erected using the pole star as a guide. Thom concluded that the builders of this miniature Stonehenge must have had a considerable degree of engineering skill and a knowledge of geometry to have constructed the site with such unerring accuracy; a suspicion that he subsequently confirmed by comparing hundreds of measurements taken from prehistoric sites all over Europe.

His research revealed another surprising fact; the discovery of a standard unit of measurement, the megalithic yard (2.72 feet), which had evidently been a constant feature in the construction of each and every site. There was no way of knowing for certain why such sites had been raised, but Thom reasoned that they were primitive observatories for predicting the eclipses of the moon.

In the 1960s Professor Gerald Hawkins, author of Stonehenge Decoded, was able to expand on Thom's theory after becoming fascinated by the fact that there were 56 huge holes in the outer ditch at Stonehenge which archaeologists were at a loss to explain. Hawkins fed astronomical data into a computer and came up with a map of the heavens as it would have been seen in the second millennium. From this he discovered that a lunar or solar eclipse occurred every 18 and a half years, whenever the winter moon was dissected by the Heel Stone. The interval is actually 18.61 years, which for practical purposes would be calculated as two times nineteen plus one eighteen year interval making a total of fifty-six – the number of the holes in the outer ditch. The priests had only to move a stone from one hole to the next to be able to calculate the next lunar eclipse. It is more than likely that the other sites served the same purpose.

Main picture: The magical site of Callanish in the Outer Hebrides, built in alignment with the sun in an 18-year cycle.

Right: Megaliths in the form of male and female symbols at Men-an-Tol near Morvah, Cornwall, England; thought to possess curative properties.

The power of the moon

The moon had great symbolic significance for primitive humans, but it may also have been a source of real power which could be harnessed at such sites and stored in the stones for ritual purposes. There is considerable evidence supporting the idea that the stones are conductors for the magnetic energy in the earth which is at its strongest during certain phases of the moon and that at those times the sites act as an amplifier.

Professor John Taylor and Dr Eduardo Balinovski, both physicists from London University, measured the magnetic field of a megalith near Crickhowell in South Wales and watched in astonishment as the needle on their gaussmeter swung violently across the dial. Further readings revealed a variation in the magnetic field at different points on the stone which other researchers have noticed reverses its polarity in accordance with the constellations. Even without expensive equipment it is possible to sensitize yourself to the power in the stones simply by touching them. A tingling feeling confirms the fact that the individual is acting as a conductor, an act which may have been practised by the High Priests of the pagan religions who in doing so would have thought of themselves as drawing up the earth's energy to vitalize the land.

The moon goddess

During research for his monumental work on the cult of the moon goddess, The White Goddess, the English poet and novelist Robert Graves discovered a sacred Druidic calendar which he believed had been in use in numerous New Stone Age cultures across Europe and which seemed to point to the possibility that the cult of the moon goddess was the core religion of the world. It was his contention that the moon goddess was the muse of art and intuition, the mistress of night and the unconscious, which in time was supplanted by the worship of the sun god, who personified the light of reason, the intellect and worldly knowledge. With the decline of the cult of the moon goddess, humanity apparently abandoned magic and the supernatural for science and religion, but at the cost of the shadow, psychic side of our nature.

Pendulum power

One of the most remarkable, but little known pioneers of psychic research was the distinguished British academic and archaeologist Professor Tom Lethbridge. He was a man who professed a healthy scepticism for all aspects of the paranormal with one exception – he had a secret passion for dowsing.

He had always been fascinated by stories of the great archaeological discoveries made by Heinrich Schliemann and Sir Arthur Evans which they had credited to an inner sixth sense, and he suspected that the dowsing, or divining rod (often a forked stick) might act as an extension of the archaeologist's intuition. He had proven the rod's potential for himself during an archaeological expedition to the island of Lundy off southwest England when he had successfully located veins of volcanic rock far underground. He was threfore keen to extend his experiments to proving the power of the pendulum, an allegedly more accurate instrument.

Dowsing experiements
At the risk of inviting ridicule from his Cambridge University colleagues, Lethbridge devoted the latter years of his life to exploring the power of the pendulum as a divining device, but during his experiments his research was to take an unexpected turn.

He had begun by placing a silver dish on the floor of his study and varying the length of string until at 56cm (22in) the pendulum began to circle. He concluded that this length must be the vibrational 'frequency' of silver and rushed out into his garden in the hope of finding a cache of buried silver coins. Holding the pendulum in one hand and with his other arm extended like an antennae he scanned the area until the pendulum indicated the direction of buried silver.

He repeated the procedure from the other side of the garden to get a second line, reasoning that where the lines crossed he would find his silver. His hopes seemed to be confirmed when the pendulum began circling over this spot. But after digging up a considerable amount of earth and a fragment of Rhineland stoneware he had found nothing of value.

When he dowsed a second time the pendulum failed to register any interest over the hole at all and Lethbridge grew despondent. But just as he was about to refill the hole he held the pendulum over the fragment of pottery and watched it go into a circular swing. It was then that he remembered that German

pottery of a particular period was often glazed with lead salts containing silver.

In a subsequent experiment he discovered that lead and silver shared the same 'vibrational frequency' which could be measured by the length of string needed to get a reaction from the pendulum. But it was possible to determine which of the two metals were being divined by the number of times the pendulum swung in a circle. For lead it circled 16 times and for silver 22.

Working on different substances
Once he had 'tuned' the pendulum into a substance it would unfailingly lead him to more of the same. On one occasion he tuned it into truffles, a rare fungus found in

Main picture: The archaeologist and academic Tom Lethbridge discovered a pendulum could be 'tuned' to specific substances and emotional states.

such delicacies as pâté de foie gras, and promptly located a specimen the size of pea which the London Science Museum analysed and declared to be an exceedingly rare variety.

Of even more interest was his discovery that human beings could 'charge' supposedly inanimate objects with their own energy and that this energy varied in vibrational rate according to the emotions of the person who handled them.

Different vibrational rates

He measured the vibrational rates of a number of sling stones that he had excavated from an Iron Age fort and which he suspected had been used in battle. The pendulum responded strongly to these at both 61cm (24in) and 102cm (40in) which he subsequently

discovered were the rates for male energy and anger.

Lethbridge discovered these correspondences in an ingenious fashion. He chose some stones from a nearby beach using a pair of tongs so that he would not influence them in any way and then he and his wife hurled them against a wall with as much force as they could muster. When they recovered the stones they discovered that all those which he had thrown reacted to a rate of 61cm (24in), while those that his wife had thrown each measured 74cm (29in). Then by holding a stone and concentrating on various abstract ideas and emotions in turn he was able to accurately measure the vibrational frequency of each using the stone as a medium.

After an exhaustive series of experiments, all of which were conscientiously repeated to make sure that the results were consistent, Lethbridge concluded that many things had the same vibrational rate, but that normally they seemed to be interconnected. For example life registered 20 as did the colour white, earth and electricity, while death registered at 40 as did the colour black, anger and sleep.

It would seem that the tables of correspondences drawn up by the ancient alchemists and magicians reflected a lost knowledge of the natural world that we are only now beginning to rediscover with the current practise of 'charging' crystals and acknowledging the innate power of stone circles.

Right: The 'traditional' form of dowsing using a forked stick.

Ley lines

At the end of the Second World War a provincial English solicitor and local councillor, Guy Underwood, retired from public service and decided to devote his remaining days to discovering the secrets of Britain's prehistoric sites. Underwood had been intrigued by the findings of Alfred Watkins, author of The Old Straight Track, who had earlier identified a network of tracks called ley lines which appeared to connect sacred sites across the country, but which he considered to be simply ancient trade routes. Underwood suspected that these tracks had a greater significance and he was determined to discover what it was, using nothing more than a simple dowsing rod.

Dowsing techniques

With the aid of a rod he confirmed the existence of underground streams and 'blind springs' at several sites that had previously been traced by two British dowsers, Captain Robert Boothby and Reginald Smith of the British Museum. Underwood's rod pulled to the left to indicate the course of the water as he had expected, but then pulled to the right to trace a more complex and precise series of geometric patterns which suggested the existence of lines of magnetic force under the earth.

The parallel lines that followed the course of the underground streams were between 30–60cm (1–2ft) apart, suggesting that this marked the extent of the energy field of the water. The second group of lines which indicated the presence and pattern of a magnetic field were consistently in the form of two sets of parallel lines like railway tracks. These were subsequently found to be either the paths used by wild animals

to forage for food and find their way back to their burrows or they marked the route of the earliest roads. This raised the possibility that primitive man was sensitive to these invisible natural forces and that consequently they built their sacred monuments where they divined reservoirs of what Underwood called geodetic force, or 'earth energy'.

Famous sacred sites

Underwood subsequently made a thorough 'survey' of Stonehenge and discovered that lines of geodetic force define the shape and features of the site itself. The outer ditch, for example, is marked by an almost complete circle with one end running northward to loop twice around the Heel Stone. The invisible lines of force also appear to have determined the outline of the famous giant chalk figures at Uffington, Cerne Abbas and

Wandlebury which had been carved into the hillsides.

Underwood concluded, 'The philosophers and priests of the old religions seemed to have believed that – particularly when manifested in spiral forms – it [the earth force] was involved with...the generative powers of Nature; that it was part of the mechanism by which what we call Life comes into being; and to have been the 'Great arranger' – that balancing principle which keeps all Nature in equilibrium...'

Geodetic forces

Underwood speculated that geodetic force is generated within the earth itself and radiates upwards in waves to exert a subtle influence on the nerve cells of all living things. It was possible that over the aeonsof time these waves left an indelible impression just below the earth's crust, just as the oceans, rivers and streams have carved features in the face of the earth's surface, and it is these repositories of the life force that have manifested in the network of energy lines which continue to have a subtle influence on our health.

The French dowser Barthelemy Bleton, for

The Uffington Horse, Oxfordshire, and Glastonbury Tor, Somerset, England, (inset) are thought to mark significant repositories of earth energy.

example, felt nauseous whenever he sat in a specific spot and only later discovered that it had been due to his 'sensitivity' to a strong underground stream. Similarly, the English writer Colin Wilson witnessed a Cornish diviner locate underground streams by interlocking the fingers of both his hands. Whenever he sensed water the diviner's hands would involuntarily pump up and down leaving him breathless and perspiring.

The idea that there is an invisible network of magnetic energy coursing through the earth to which we are all sensitive to different degrees is not a new one. The ancient Chinese saw the earth's current as the negative and positive expressions of yin and yang and went to extraordinary lengths to channel the energy by placing pagodas at key locations to act as pointed conductors. They applied the same principle to the practice of acupuncture where the flow of vital energy in the human body is stimulated by placing needles at key junctions.

Gaia – the living planet

Gaia is the name that the ancient Greeks gave to the Earth goddess who, in common with the capricious female deities of many early pagan religions, was envisaged as being protective and maternal but also capable of considerable cruelty. Those who worshipped her would be nurtured and blessed with bountiful harvests, plentiful rainfall and fertility, while those who turned their back on Mother Earth would be scourged by the raging elements and suffer famine and disease.

When British scientist James Lovelock formulated his theory of the Earth as a living entity in the 1960s it seemed appropriate for him to adopt the name of the goddess to convey the idea that there would be fearful consequences if we continued to recklessly plunder the planet's resources and wilfully poison the environment.

Lovelock had long been fascinated by the fact that the Earth does not conform to the accepted laws of physics. For example, there should be a much higher concentration of salt in our rivers after aeons of water corrosion than there is at present. Something has regulated the level to sustain the fresh water ecosystem. Likewise, the atmosphere does not contain as much carbon dioxide from exhaust fumes and industrial pollutants as scientists expected. According to the laws of thermodynamics the Earth should now be entirely uninhabitable, but it is teeming with life.

A living entity

The possibility that the earth was a living entity which sustained and nurtured life came to Lovelock in a flash of insight similar to those experienced by mystics who momentarily glimpse a greater reality, and it appeared to confirm what these visionaries had known for centuries. But Lovelock was acutely aware that such a radical idea would have to be backed by sound scientific evidence if it was to be taken seriously by the academic establishment, and so he teamed up with the distinguished biologist Lynn Margulis to ensure that his research had the broadest possible base. Initially, they cautiously described their hypothesis in terms of life determining its environment, rather than the reverse: 'Life, or the biosphere, regulates or maintains the climate and the atmospheric composition at an optimum for itself.'

A self-regulating system

But as the evidence accumulated they were forced to modify the theory. While they stopped short of stating that the Earth is a conscious sentient being, as many in the New Age movement maintain, they were able to prove conclusively that the planet is not a lump of inanimate rock which chance has favoured with life. This had been the accepted view among orthodox scientists who, to Lovelock's frustration, continue to think of the Earth in terms of distinct spheres of influence arbitrarily divided into the biosphere, the atmosphere, the lithosphere and the hydrosphere. Rather it

Left: British scientist, James Lovelock, formulated the theory of the Earth as a living entity.

is a single self-regulating, self-sustaining physiological system. It is alive to the same extent that any living organism is alive in that it regulates its chemistry and temperature and is active in the cycle of life, death and regeneration.

Lovelock likens it to a tree that is continually, but imperceptibly interacting with the sunlight and the soil to grow and change. He envisages Gaia as an evolving system that has emerged from the reciprocal evolution of organisms and their environment, but is clear that the self-regulation of climate and chemical composition are entirely automatic. 'Self-regulation emerges as the system evolves. No foresight, planning or teleology (suggestion of design or purpose in nature) are involved.'

He distrusts the extremist environmentalist view that humans have become a 'leukaemia' of the Earth, an alien organism that has run out of control and is threatening the entire ecosystem. We are instead to be seen as an integral element of the system who are at least conscious of the consequences of disturbing the harmony to which the Earth is attuned. And he suggests that acid rain, the greenhouse effect and other planetary problems might not be harbingers of disaster to be visited upon us by an irate goddess, but rather symptoms of the planet's growing pains.

According to Lovelock we do not have to understand the causes of our current climactic and environmental crisis to begin to effect a cure. So long as we see the symptoms we should act to contain its

Above: According to orthodox science, the Earth should be uninhabitable by now, but it is evidently a self-sustaining physiological system.

effects. Later, when we have the insight or technology we can learn how we manage to seal the hole in the ozone layer or reduce acid rain. He likens our current situation to the Romans who knew that living on wetlands was unhealthy and so they drained the marshes. They did not understand that the marshlands were breeding grounds for mosquitoes who transmitted the malaria parasite and they didn't wait to find out that that was the case. We too should act now to apply what he calls 'planetary medicine' to our sick planet before it is too late.

Channelling

From early times self-proclaimed prophets have claimed to commune directly with God. Mystics have also spoken of hearing a still, small voice within and mediums have passed on messages from the dead or their own spirit guides. More recently the lines of communication have been extended to other planets from where highly evolved beings are said to be 'channelling' urgent messages for the future welfare of humans, if the claims of a growing number of psychic 'transceivers' are to be believed.

Since the 1970s there has been a significant increase in these channelled teachings due, it is claimed, to the downloading of cosmic energy which will initiate the beginning of the New Age. It would be tempting to dismiss such pronouncements as the delusions of highly imaginative individuals who are eager to achieve a certain celebrity by publishing their 'communications', if it was not for the striking similarity of the messages which have been received as far apart as the USA, India and Australia. If even a small proportion of these telepathic teachings are genuine then we will be in for a worldwide awakening to a far greater reality than we are prepared to acknowledge at present.

Channelled messages

Barbara Marciniak, a trance channeller from North Carolina in the USA, presents her received wisdom in the language of a New Age philosopher. According to Marciniak's intergalactic guru in the Pleiades Planetary system, we and our galactic brethren are all members of a 'Family of Light' who have to energize our inner selves through positive

Left: 'Wreckage' from the Pleiadean UFO crash at Roswell, USA was revealed to be a fragment of a weather balloon. Transceivers maintain this was a typical government 'cover up'.

thought and eliminate non-dynamic words such as 'should' and 'try' from our vocabularies.

Apparently, it is only by learning to 'go beyond fear' that we will consciously create the 'new reality' and the 'new Earth' for the New Age. Her first book, Bringers Of The Dawn – Teachings from the Pleiadians, allegedly compiled from 400 hours of channelling, reads like a management strategist's handbook, with Jesus described as a 'systems buster'!

The main American guru of channelled Pleiadian philosophy is Barbara Hand Clow, an astrological counsellor and authority on Native American ceremonies and sacred sites. She has written innumerable books on cosmic evolution, new consciousness and the blossoming sub-genre known as 'speculative visionary work', or channelling.

Clow claims that her first contact with the Pleiadians occurred when she was just four months old when the curtain next to her crib was blown aside to reveal 'beautiful small blue beings'. Later, as an adult, she began to receive telepathic messages in Morse code before they finally filtered through as intelligible transmissions.

'I have to admit, this was not an easy time for me,' she candidly explains in the preface to The Pleiadian Agenda. 'It was often very psychologically complex because the more I got to know the Pleiadians, the more I realized that their voice was actually my own inner child voice ... forcing me to remember my true and non-imprinted natal self.'

Believable channelling

So much unbelievable information has been written by self-styled transceivers who seem unable to discriminate between spiritual truths from a genuine cosmic source and spurious speculations from their own subconscious that it's no surprise most people dismiss the whole idea of channelling. However, there are some truly revelationary books of received wisdom to be found, and one of the best

is: The Only Planet of Choice by Phyllis V. Schlemmer and Mary Bennett.

For 20 years Schlemmer, an American transceiver, and a group of scientists and spiritual seekers, which included Star Trek creator Gene Roddenberry, claimed to be in regular contact with a benign being to whom they gave the rather prosaic name of 'Tom'.

Tom identified himself as a member of a group of highly evolved, discarnate spirits of pure energy and infinite intelligence whose purpose is to balance the forces of the Universe. Tom explained that, while the inhabitants of other planets do have choice, the consciousness is collective. Only on Earth can a being exercise free will and experience individual choice.

Earth, we are told, is a school for the soul, and one of the most difficult lessons we have to learn is discrimination. By raising our consciousness we will all be able to make contact with highly evolved beings who can accelerate our evolution. But we must understand that not all extraterrestrial civilizations are in advance of our own. Some have an equally limited understanding of the universe as we do, while others are to be considered negative. We should also be wary of those among us who claim to have exclusive access to the 'Truth', be they religious leaders, politicians or extra-terrestrial transceivers.

Main picture: The Pleiades constellation from where many extra-terrestrial communications are said to originate.

'A Son of God can recognize his power in one instant and change the world in the next. That is because, by changing his mind, he has changed the most powerful device that was ever given him for change.'

This truism is taken from one of the most widely published and intensely studied of the channelled texts – A Course In Miracles, a three-volume self-study course which devotees claim will alter the reader's perception of reality. Its central theme is encapsulated in the opening quotation, 'Nothing real can be threatened. Nothing unreal exists.'

Incredibly, the anonymous text has inspired other accompanying literature, mostly commentaries in which the avid disciples describe the Course as: 'the direct Thoughts of God' brought into being to awaken man from his own illusions.

A way of life

They claim that it is not to be simply read and understood but to be lived. And that it offers us a choice which, in this age of increasing materialism and violence, we cannot afford to postpone.

One section says: 'Where you come to the place where the branch in the road is quite apparent, you cannot go ahead. You must go either one way or the other ... The whole purpose of coming this far was to decide which branch you will take now. The way you came no longer matters.'

Although essentially Christian in tone and content it was allegedly 'dictated' to a Jewish research psychologist at Columbia University in New York. It might be significant to note that the 'medium' in this case was a psychologist as the subliminal message of the Course seems to be that debilitating fears emanate from the ego while inner wisdom is the voice of the unconscious. The fact that the medium was inspired by an inner voice also suggests that, in this case at least, the source might not have been a discarnate spirit but her own Higher Self.

Messages for the millennium?

Whatever the true origins of these channelled teachings might be and their value to humanity, the question remains: why did so many of them appear in the 1980s and 1990s? Could it be that the symbolic significance of the new Millennium and the many apocryphal predictions made for the year 2000 stimulated the over-active imaginations of these new prophets, or were we really being prepared for a spiritual regeneration?

The mystics remind us that there is an Eternal Law which states that a need must be met and that even if we are not consciously aware of it, our desire for a better world is now bringing down the means by which we can achieve it.

In contrast to the quiet wisdom recorded in A Course in Miracles are the apocalyptic prophecies revealed to a group of New Age seekers known as the Ramala Group during their regular meditation meetings at Glastonbury, England.

Over a ten-year period, from the mid-1970s, the group claimed to have made telepathic contact with highly

Main picture: New Age teachings often urge us to choose our own path and not concern ourselves with the past or regrets about what we leave behind.

sensitivity to the spiritual realms) to escape the flood of negative forces which will sweep aside all our carefully crafted illusions.

'...the Lord of this Earth, the Goddess, the Earth Mother whose form it is, is a great and evolved spiritual being...It will, therefore, never die...its physical form might change as it experiences periods of transformation and transmutation...in the same way that you in your physical bodies die and are born again onto a higher plane of life so the Earth, on another level undergoes a similar experience' (transmission from the Ramala Teachers).

So apparently, Planet Earth is also destined for rebirth in the coming centuries as it continues to evolve along with the life forms it sustains.

Below: Every day of our lives and on every level we are constantly being forced to make choices and decisions.

evolved spiritual beings and to have channelled their prophecies in preparation for the 'transformation and transmutation' that will instigate the coming Aquarian age (which some say has already begun and others anticipate in the 21st century). This era is destined to be the most significant cycle in humanity's evolutionary path, even more so than the current Piscean Age which the Ramala contacts predict is to come to a violent end.
These beings have warned that humanity is ill-prepared for the great planetary changes to come and that if we are to survive this infusion of cosmic energy we must build an 'ark of consciousness', (ie. a general raising of awareness and

The New Age gurus

In the 1960s the youth of the western world fell under the spell of the teachings of Maharishi Mahesh Yogi, the 'Giggling Guru' whose spiritual mission was first sponsored by The Beatles. In the 1980s, after the Maharishi had returned to the Himalayas, his role was effectively taken over by an equally charismatic and considerably more controversial figure, Bhagwan Shree Rajneesh (1931–90), more popularly known as Osho.

To his followers Osho was worshipped as 'the greatest spiritual teacher of the twentieth century', but his critics insisted that he was the leader of an insidious cult and derided him.

Even since his death several years ago, the personality cult which developed around this enigmatic Indian with a passion for collecting Rolls Royce cars has shown no signs of abatting. Every year thousands of devoted disciples flock to the his large landscaped commune that he established in Poona, India.

Osho's legacy

Osho left 600 titles containing his teachings which were dutifully transcribed by his inner circle from discourses and discussions that he had given to audiences around the world. In these he is said to have liberated universal truths from the dogma of orthodox religion, condensed the convoluted philosophies of the Eastern mystics and made both much more comprehensible to a new generation.

He saw himself as the forerunner of a new race of enlightened, more spiritually aware beings with a lusty love of life that he jokingly called 'Zorba the Buddha'.

'The new man is not a hope: you are already pregnant with it', he once announced.' My work is just to make you aware that the new man has already arrived. My work is to help you to recognize and respect him...from fish to man there has been evolution. But from man to a Buddha, from man to a Christ, from man to a Kabir [the Indian mystic], it is not evolution it is revolution.'

He envisaged the New Age as an era free from religious constraints and political pragmatism, an era far more beautiful and fulfilling than the artists and visionaries could ever have imagined.

Osho also said: 'As far as I can see, Zen is going to be paving the path for the new man to come, and for the new humanity to emerge...Zen is a way of dissolving philosophical problems, not of solving them. It is a way of getting rid of philosophy, because philosophy is a sort of neurosis...The greatest thing that Zen has brought into the world is freedom from oneself.'

His main hope was that people would throw away the crutches of orthodox religion and blind faith in favour of the intuitive way of life of Zen Buddhism.

Mother Meera

Devotees of Mother Meera, a young Indian woman who receives pilgrims from all over the world to her modest home in the village of Dornburg-Thalheim, Germany, for a nightly blessing do not think of her simply as a guru. For them she is more than human. She is what the Hindus call an avatar, an incarnation of an aspect of the Divine, in this instance the Mother Goddess, the feminine principle.

Her blessing, which is freely given without exception to all who make the journey, takes place in reverential silence and lasts for about two hours. She makes no pronouncements, but simply lays her hands for a few moments on each individual in turn and then looks intently into their eyes.

It is said that in this moment she is looking directly into the soul and that she channels energy to wherever it is needed. By laying on her hands she is also thought to untie the knots in the invisible veins running through the etheric body which can become entangled and block the free flow of energy around the body. The effects of this 'clearing' process and of being in her presence are different with each individual, but are said to be subtle and profound.

Evolution and change

'The possibility for mankind to evolve and change is always there whether or not an avatar comes,' she has explained in one of several books to be written by her disciples. 'People naturally believe in a greater reality. However, when an avatar comes people feel the possibility more and aspire more strongly...The consciousness of mankind is being prepared for great leaps and discoveries...This leap is certain. It will happen. It is happening now ...transcendence, union with the divine, is the primary aim of the human being. The goal of the divine personality, or avatar, is to help the human being to be in the divine...I have not come only to be a refuge; I have also come to give the joy and strength necessary for change.'

Even if the possibility of a supernatural exchange of energy is ruled out in such cases, the very act of commitment to something which promises increased self-awareness, seems to make an impression on the unconscious and effects a change in consciousness.

Main picture: Bhagwan Shree Rajneesh, popularly known as Osho, offers spiritual sustenance to devoted followers.

For the average person the term 'New Age' has become a fashionable and convenient label to describe a proliferation of exotic practises, complementary therapies, alternative lifestyles and off-beat philosophies which appear unconventional and perhaps even eccentric.

This unfortunate misconception, which is based on the trivialization of the movement's more unorthodox ideas, has obscured a subtle but significant development in the way an increasing number of people are now viewing the world and their part in it.

In this holistic world-view, technological advances and materialism are no longer seen as primary considerations, but as secondary to the quality of life and fulfilment of everyone's potential. The relentless pursuit of material comfort and the amassing of possessions is regarded as potentially dehumanising when pursued at the expense of spiritual wellbeing. New Age practises aim to empower the individual to be more self-contained, to realize their full potential and to accept that the only way they can change the world is to change themselves first.

Ancient traditions

It is a view which is consistent with both the Eastern esoteric tradition, which makes each of us responsible for our own

spiritual development, and with the theories of western psychology which assists the individual towards self-realization. It also updates our ancestors' belief that the earth is a living entity and as such is a matrix of cosmic energy to which we can sensitize ourselves.

New Age movement

We tend to think of the New Age movement as a development of the hippie idealism of the late 1960s when Western youth attempted to 'go back to the garden' having 'turned on, tuned in and dropped out' on the advice of Dr Timothy Leary. Leary, the radical American psychologist, advocated the expansion of consciousness through the use of psychedelic drugs, while other gurus of the Californian counter-culture, such as British born Alan Watts, saw meditation, in combination with a return to a more natural lifestyle, as the only credible alternative.

It was Watts' belief that to initiate the New Age, each of us has to realize that we are instruments of creation and not separate, that we all originate from a common source. We are all unique manifestations of the 'One' (God) who has taken many diverse forms in order to express itself fully. Once we are reconciled to our twofold nature we will bring the New Age into being as effortlessly as the plant emerges from the seed, without having to wait upon the blessings of providence.

During the heady days of the late Sixties the New Age was linked in the popular imagination with astrology and

the Age of Aquarius, but it soon became evident that planetary transformation was dependent upon a change in human consciousness and not upon celestial configurations.

In the Seventies hippie idealism matured into the more realistic aims of the human potential movement which advocated an holistic approach to personal growth and self-actualization, combined with various bodywork techniques for improved physical and psychological health.

At the forefront of this activity was one of the founding fathers of the New Age movement, the late Sir George Trevelyan. In 1969 Trevelyan had set up a Trust in Hertfordshire offering courses in 'New Age consciousness' to prepare people for the physical and spiritual crisis to come.

'Armageddon is indeed being fought out within human hearts,' he once wrote, 'outward events merely mirror the condition of the soul.'

He saw the increase in crime and social deprivation as an essential part of a cleansing process which is necessary to rid us of the accumulated debris of centuries of selfishness and greed. And he attributed the increase in natural disasters to the wholesale plundering and polluting of the earth's resources.

According to Trevelyan, our evolution follows the pattern of nature in which growth requires the disintegration of dead and decaying matter before new life can spring forth. It was his conclusion that the advent of the New Age is as inevitable as the cycle of the seasons.

The Celestine Prophecy

Since the 1970s the increased interest in alternative lifestyles, complementary health programmes and self-help systems has coincided with a general dissatisfaction in traditional religious beliefs, to the point where there is now a considerable demand for what might be called spiritual guidance books. Through a lively mix of Eastern philosophy, western psychological principles and practical advice, the authors of these books have sought to bring meaning and purpose to the confusion of modern life. People have avidly read their words and these authors have now acquired a form of cult status as New Age gurus (see page 56).

Few of these writers, however, have enjoyed the worldwide popularity of American sociologist and counsellor James Redfield whose positive philosophy was crystallized in the multi-million selling The Celestine Prophecy and its many sequels. What makes Redfield's book unique is that he has simplified rather complex concepts into nine key insights into the meaning of life and integrated them into a spiritual adventure story.

Spiritual evolution

The fictional plot concerns the discovery of an ancient Peruvian manuscript and its subsequent suppression by the Church. The contents of this sacred document and the secrets that it contains are revealed piece by piece to the central character through apparently coincidental meetings with various strangers who have each been privileged to see a part of the manuscript.

Each person discloses a different insight into the course of human spiritual evolution as revealed by the manuscript, but only when the author has reached the stage of development where he is ready to ask the appropriate question. In this respect the story echoes the ancient maxim which promises that

Left: Our spiritual revolution is dependent upon accepting the fact that our negative emotions cause dis-ease at all levels. This shows the astral body of the irritable person.

Author James Redfield and other New Age gurus predict that the Earth will become a new Garden of Eden.

'the teacher will appear when the pupil is ready'. In other words, we will all be taught what we need to know about life when we have reached the level of awareness that prompts us to seek the answer.

The nine insights

The first insight is that each and every incident in our lives is part of a universal plan and as such serves a specific purpose. Events that we perceive as just being coincidences are in fact contrived to awaken us to our part in the play that we call life. We have the free will to recognize these signs that are intended to guide us along our true path so that we can realize our purpose and potential. Alternatively, we can ignore them and continue to sleepwalk through life.

The second insight predicts that at the turn of the year 2000 humanity will become aware of its purpose and ultimate destiny so that it will not want to repeat the mistakes of the past.

The third insight reveals that part of the evolutionary process involves an increasing awareness of the universal energies that pervade the universe and the development of our psychic sensitivity.

The fourth insight warns that while humanity as a whole

becomes increasingly aware of its divine destiny there is a contrary impulse in human nature that will compel some people to undermine our evolutionary progress by trying to control and dominate those they see as being weaker.

The fifth insight states that we all have the ability to draw upon the universal life force at will and that this limitless source of energy not only sustains us but can also heal our mind, body and spirit.

The sixth insight suggests that many of our problems stem from our habit of trying to enforce our will upon other people, a habit which derives from the attention seeking techniques that we used in childhood. If we are to evolve as a species we will have to mature from this childhood stage to the adult by becoming less self-centred and prey to our passions.

The seventh insight develops this idea of our spiritual growth mirroring the stages of life by stating that we need to become self-reliant and self-aware rather than depending on the approval or support of other people to define who we really are.

If we can develop this level of awareness and sense of self we will find that the mysteries of life and death will be revealed to us through intuition and insight. We will learn why

we were born into a particular family and what lessons are to be learnt in this life. The younger generation are already becoming conscious of this truth, which explains the increase in interest in alternative therapies and beliefs which in turn draws down more energy and accelerates the evolutionary process.

The penultimate insight states that we are all an indispensable element in the evolution of the human species.

The ninth insight describes the changes in human consciousness and the global community that can come about in the coming centuries which are the result of bringing to conscious awareness these universal truths. There can be a new sense of values that will lead to the rejection of the consumer society which will be replaced with a 'spiritual economy' in which no one will prosper at another person's expense. In addition, the current culture of fear that places undue emphasis on science to provide all the solutions and work to save us from starvation will evaporate because no one will feel the need to amass material possessions. Ultimately science and spirituality will be reconciled and the earth will become a new Garden of Eden.

CHAPTER 3

FORESEEING THE FUTURE

There is a wealth of anecdotal evidence to support the belief that we all share an innate sixth sense which gives us the potential to foresee future events (precognition). But it is also known that these insights are normally confined to our dreams when the rational mind is sleeping and the latent psychic faculties are free to filter through from the subconscious mind.

But even if we accept precognition as a fact, the questions remain. Does it mean that we are merely the puppets of fate, and that our lives are predetermined before we are even born? Or do we always possess free will to alter the future that is foreseen? Carl Jung, the founder of modern psychoanalysis, concluded that the true value of predicting the future with divinatory tools such as the I Ching, tarot cards or runes had nothing to do with prophecy and the paranormal, but was from their ability to amplify the inner voice of the subconscious mind that everybody possesses.

Main picture: A crystal ball has no powers in itself, but serves as a focus for the psychic sensitivity of the person using it.

Prophecy and prediction

Jeanne Dixon, the 'High Society seer', became an American talk show celebrity after predicting the assassination of John F. Kennedy 11 years before the event occurred in 1963. She foresaw the president's death in a vision of the then unknown politician standing outside the White House with the date 1960 clearly visible, just like the opening credits of a movie. An inner voice informed her that a democrat would be elected President in 1960 and assassinated while in office.

Further predictions
After the president's death, Dixon had another prophetic vision which foretold tragedy for the Kennedy family. This time her warnings that the younger brother Edward would suffer serious injury in a plane crash reached the ears of the family, but they evidently chose to ignore her. The next day Edward was almost crippled when his private plane crashed just as Jeanne had predicted.

However, her most dramatic pronouncement concerning the Kennedys occurred in front of hundreds of witnesses during a public appearance at the Ambassador Hotel, Los Angeles in May 1968. Someone in the audience asked about Robert Kennedy's presidential prospects to which Jeanne replied: 'He will never be President because of a tragedy that will take place right here in this hotel.' A week later Robert Kennedy was assassinated by a gunman as he was led through the kitchen of the Ambassador Hotel.

Nostradamus
The most famous prophet of all though is unquestionably Nostradamus (1503–66), also known as the Seer of Salon, who was apparently able to foresee events so far into the future that he could not possibly have understood the implications of what he described. His ambiguous and cryptic descriptions are a source of intense speculation to this day and are open to a number of contrasting interpretations. In common with a number of other seers and psychics, Nostradamus correctly predicted the date of his own death. But more remarkably, he even foresaw the date he would be reinterred – 134 years later!

He was buried with a metal plate engraved with the year which he had predicted he would be exhumed. One hundred and thirty-four years later the authorities decided to place the prophet's remains in a more prominent position, but before they reburied it they opened the coffin to make sure the corpse was indeed that of their most celebrated citizen. The skeleton was identified as that of Nostradamus, but as if to satisfy those who doubted his prophetic gifts the metal plate confirmed the date of this most bizarre event – the year 1700.

Edgar Cayce
However, not all prophets predict disaster. Edgar Cayce (1877–1945), one of America's most celebrated seers, was known as 'The Sleeping Prophet' due to his habit of lapsing into a dream-like state from which he could accurately

Main picture: American psychic and celebrity seer Jeanne Dixon who correctly predicted the death and disaster of the Kennedy clan.

Right: Nostradamus predicted a global apocalypse would take place in 1999, but correctly foresaw the date of his own death and reinterment.

diagnose a patient's illness without them even being present.

Often the cures he prescribed were obscure compounds which only a specialist practitioner would have known. On one notable occasion he even prescribed a drug that the company had named only an hour before!

Although Cayce declared that he had no interest in gaining financially from his gift, he saw nothing wrong in allowing others to profit from his unerringly accurate financial forecasts.

In March 1929, and again the following month, he warned an investor that the value of stocks and shares would plummet and remain at an all time low for some considerable time. Cayce's prediction was proved correct by the Wall Street Crash of late October when 29 million shares were sold over five days in a financial panic which was to lead to wholesale bankruptcy, massive unemployment and the Great Depression.

Cayce was convinced that he owed his psychic insights to his ability to put his conscious mind 'to sleep' and to allow his unconscious to tap into the universal mind or Collective Consciousness, as he called it. It was his belief that the pattern of future events is already predetermined, but that the free will that everyone has, determines the final details and timings.

The tarot and the tree of life

Legend has it that the tarot cards, one of most popular fortune-telling devices in use today, originated on the 'lost continent' of Atlantis. The island's high priests are said to have designed the deck as a means of preserving their secrets in symbolic form shortly before the catalclysm which sent their advanced civilization to the bottom of the ocean.

Unfortunately, this colourful tale is not borne out by the facts. The oldest surviving tarot cards date from the 15th century and no earlier versions are known to exist. The fact that the cards have also been found to conform to Kabbalistic principles in a form which is characteristic of medieval Europe also suggests that they are not of great antiquity, although the wisdom teachings which they embody certainly date back to the origins of the western esoteric tradition.

The major and minor arcana

The 78 card deck of tarot cards is comprised of four suits (most commonly named Wands, Swords, Cups and Pentacles) corresponding to each of the four worlds of Kabbalistic tradition. Each suit has ten numbered cards, one for each of the sephirah (see Kabbalah page 20) which symbolize the divine attributes on the Tree of Life, and four court cards (King, Queen, Knight and Page) personifying the four elements of fire, air, water and earth within each of these realms. In psychological terms these four elements correspond to our intuition, intellect, emotions and the senses. Together the numbered cards and the court cards are known as the minor arcana.

In addition, there are 22 picture cards known as the major arcana which correspond to the 22 paths connecting the sephiroth on the Tree of Life.

The archetypal characters and the scenes portrayed on these cards are commonly interpreted as signifying the people who will have an influence on the life of the person for whom the cards are being read, and the incidents which will arise if events take their present course.

In contrast, the Kabbalistic tradition, which forbids fortune-telling, views the major arcana as symbolic of the stages in every person's life from an innocent in the World, personified by The Fool, to the fully realized and integrated personality represented by the Magician who is depicted with the symbols of the four elements at his command. The events are then seen not as experiences arbitarily dealt by Fate, but as the inevitable consequences of our predictable actions, provided that we act according to type.

How the cards work

The tarot has proved to be enduringly popular over the centuries because of the uncanny accuracy of its psychological insights and its apparent ability to foretell future events. And yet not even professional tarot readers are certain how it works. The belief is that while the pack is being shuffled by the person who has requested the reading they are unconsciously selecting the significant cards that are destined to be dealt. This is too incredible for the rational mind to accept and yet, the validity and accuracy of the system is difficult to dismiss.

Those who view the cards as a focus for their intuition, rather than as a divinatory device, would rather believe that the cards are shuffled and selected at random, as in a normal card game, but that being based on universal principles and common character traits the selection of cards is not uniquely significant. Whichever cards are dealt they will all be relevant for whoever requests the reading. However, the accuracy of the reading and the amount of information the reader is able to give while meditating on the symbols will depend on their intuitive abilities and not any supernatural agencies possessed by the cards.

For this reason anyone can learn to use the cards to explore their own psyche and to develop greater self-awareness or to seek guidance to specific questions at crucial moments in their life.

Although it is valid to use the picture cards as meditational gateways to specific areas of the astral plane equated with the paths on the Tree of Life, the practical value of the tarot is as a focus for our own intuition and insights into the psyche.

Tarot – mirror of the psyche

These two pages are ideal for helping the beginner to become familiar with the symbols of the major and minor arcana and for helping to prove the validity of the tarot to use yourself.

Guidance

First, shuffle the cards thoroughly, then shuffle them once again while asking each of the questions listed below. After you have considered each question place the top card and seven further cards in the position and order indicated. Then trust to your intuition to provide the answers using the key to the cards as an initial stimulus.

2 3 4 5 6 7 8

1

Questions

1. What are the most significant influences in my life at this moment?
2. What are my real aspirations?
3. What is the primary issue that I need to resolve in order to fulfil my life's purpose?
4. What do I need to understand more fully to help me in this life?
5. How can I overcome any difficulties I may encounter?
6. What can I do to make the most of the guidance I have been given?
7. What general guidance is offered for my future happiness?
8. What is my true potential?

The calender spread

This simple exercise uses only the cards of the major arcana which are to be shuffled and then dealt out in a clockwise direction to form a circle.

The card at the position of 'one o'clock' represents the influences at work in the current month, the card at 'two o'clock' indicates the character of the month to come and so on through the coming year until '12 o'clock' gives a indication for what will be happening this time next year.

Initially the key words associated with each of the cards as given below will be sufficient to give a reading, but more detailed and intuitive readings will come with practise and further study of the symbols.

Key to the cards – the minor arcana

Wands (the suit of ideas and aspirations)
Ace Fulfilment
II Wisdom
III Understanding
IV Unexpected good fortune
V Indecision
VI Accomplishment
VII Struggle for self-determination
VIII Trust to instinct
IX Learning through a difficult experience
X Wilfulness

Swords (the suit of the intellect)
Ace Insight
II Intuition
III Sentiment
IV Remembrance
V Reason

VI Responsibility
VII Evasion, self-deception
VIII Loss of direction, self-defeating
IX Irrational fears, coming to terms with loss
X End of illusions

Cups (the suit of the emotions)
Ace Unconditional love
II Harmony, sharing
III Joy, friendship
IV Ingratitude and reliance on luck
V Acceptance of loss
VI Magnanimity
VII Temptation, the danger of self-delusion
VIII Discrimination
IX Self satisfaction
X Affection and consideration

Pentacles (the suit relating to domestic and career concerns)
Ace Prosperity and new opportunities
II Stability through flexibility
III Mastery of craft or career through greater understanding
IV The need for grounding oneself in the present
V Fear of failure
VI The need for generosity
VII Reaping the rewards of past efforts
VIII A period of learning
IX A period of leisure
X A period for questioning perceptions

The four court cards in each suit can be interpreted as corresponding to the following characteristics:
King of Batons – Strong will and imagination
Queen of Batons – Empathic,

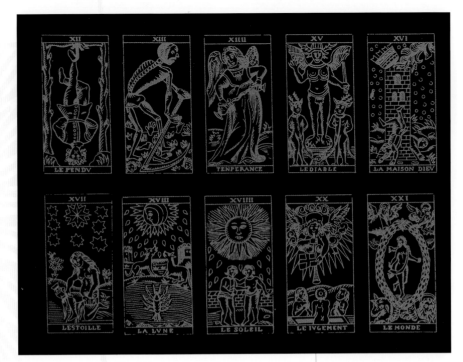

Above: A suit of tarot trumps from the Rider-Waite deck—the most popular in use today and the easiest pack for the beginner to work with.

understanding
Knight of Batons – Far-sighted, shrewd
Page of Batons – Decisive and determined
King of Swords – Maturity, integrity
Queen of Swords – A person of principle, faithful, patient
Knight of Swords – Prolific, impetuous, inspired
Page of Swords – Curious, independent and self-sufficient
King of Cups – Restraint. Controlled emotions but a passionate nature
Queen of Cups – Devoted, responsible, compassionate
Knight of Cups – Love of life, idealistic and enthusiastic
Page of Cups – Romantic, loyal, supportive
King of Pentacles – Worldly wisdom and experience
Queen of Pentacles – Prudent, productive, practical and protective
Knight of Pentacles – Ambitious, energetic, reliable
Page of Pentacles – Sensual nature, restless for success and recognition

Key to the cards – the major arcana

The Wheel of Fortune – Karma
The Fool – Free will and self-determination.
The World – Discernment
The Devil – Self-deception, indulgence, wilfulness and enslavement
The Tower – Illusions, false pride and ill-conceived ambition.
The Lovers – Passion
The Hanged Man – Self-doubt and indecision.
The Hermit – The search for self-awareness
The Star – Intuition and the guiding inner light leading to self-knowledge
The Sun –The love of life and worldly wisdom
The Moon – The awakening of psychic and intuitive powers and the need for reflection
Temperance – Restraint and moderation, the need for forgiveness and self-discipline
The High Priest (The Hierophant) – Faith in a positive outcome and strength

of one's convictions leading to wisdom
The High Priestess – Insight and understanding
Death – The need for change.
The Magician – Integration of all aspects of the personality and control over one's own life
The Emperor – Fulfillment of the masculine principle in both the male and female personality
The Empress – Fulfilment of the feminine principle
Judgement – Compassion
Justice – Responsibility
Chariot – Triumph, control
Strength – Self-discipline

Runes

The runes, whose name derives from a word in the ancient northern European language meaning 'a secret', are becoming an increasingly popular form of divination. In a sense they are similar to the tarot cards in that the greater knowledge the reader has of the symbols the more expansive will be the answers and insights they can gain from a reading. However, the runes are easier for the beginner to work with as there are only 24 runic symbols that you need to become familiar with.

Although legend has it that the runes were a gift from the Norse god Odin, the symbols appear to be a composite of Bronze Age carvings, the German runic alphabet and Greek and Latin letters. They are to be found on ancient monuments and ritual artefacts across Europe as well as carved on the prows of Viking ships, which suggests that they were used primarily to invoke the protection of the gods.

Casting the runes

Each symbol is inscribed on a flattened pebble and carried in a pouch from which the sitter chooses a number of pebbles to be 'cast', having first formulated a question. A reading can be made using just a single rune for a simple 'yes' or 'no' answer, or more can be cast to give a more detailed picture of the sitter's current situation, temperament and potential for the future.

For example, much can be revealed by a three stone spread which will sum up the current situation, the necessary action to be taken and the likely outcome when read from left to right.

Simple readings

In a simple reading, such as the single or three stone spread, the runes are picked out of the bag and placed on a table before the reader, but for more complex readings a total of nine runes might be cast, three at a time, into a sacred circle or grid. Those that fall

outside the marked area are considered to be irrelevant to the reading and are ignored as are those which fall face down. Runes which land face up but upside down, facing away from the reader, are considered to have a reverse meaning.

An alternative method is to stand over the circle and simply empty the bag over it.

The sacred grid

This is created by casting three rows of three runes in the following order:

These can either be drawn out of the bag one at a time in the manner of a 'lucky dip' and placed in the order indicated, or thrown one at a time onto a grid that has been drawn on a

Left: The runes can either be picked 'lucky dip' style out of a bag, or 'cast' in a circle and significance given to the way they fall.

piece of card. Those that fall outside the grid or across a line are returned to the bag and the casting continued until there is a rune in each of the nine spaces.

The runes can then be read either diagonally, horizontally or vertically.

Traditionally, the three horizontal rows were considered to be governed by the three Fates which would be interpreted by a modern reader as meaning that the lower row would be concerned with past events, the middle row with the present and the top row with the future.

However, the Nordic tradition does not see the future as written in the stones, but as a continually evolving pattern which is woven strand by strand by our present actions. As with the tarot, the runes are not dictating our present or future actions, but rather revealing the circumstances which we have created for ourselves and indicating the means by which we can resolve any problems.

Interpreting the symbols

Unlike the tarot, runes do not have striking pictures to stimulate the unconscious and so if you are doing a reading for yourself you will have to find the significance of the symbols in a book. But with practise the standard definitions will act only as an initial stimulus. As you begin to trust your intuition you should find deeper layers of meaning without having to consult a book.

The symbols are ideographic which means that behind each sound is a concept. For example, Uruz represents both the sound 'U' and the horned cattle known as auroch, to give a divinatory meaning which suggests endurance, stubbornness and strength.

Equally important however, is the way that the stones fall if they are cast at random into a circle. If they fall in a group it suggests that they are to be considered together as pieces in a single picture, whereas if they land in a scattered pattern it implies that there are several issues that need to be taken into account.

Main picture: The Rok rune stone, discovered in Sweden in the 1940s, is covered with 800 runic letters.

Astrology

Few subjects polarize people's opinion more passionately than astrology. It is arguably the most ancient of the esoteric arts and the one that most people are familiar with through the daily horoscopes printed in the national newspapers. However, it is also the most misunderstood and misused subject. For every serious astrologer there are dozens who have only a superficial understanding of the art and whose use of its principles for prediction is a corruption of the tradition.

Astrology's two central premises state that correlations exist between celestial and terrestrial events and that the position of the planets at the moment of a person's birth has a direct influence on their personality and the way they lead their lives.

How astrology works

Sceptics would argue that distant planetary bodies can't possibly exercise influence over human beings and they cite the astrologers use of an erroneous but necessary device to make their calculations compute. In astrology the Sun and Moon are counted among the planets and the Earth is seen as the centre of the Solar system.

Astrologers know this to be technically incorrect, but justify it by arguing that the planetary alignments are merely symbolic of a pattern of energy present in the universe at the time of a person's birth and that the characteristics of the major planets are convenient symbols for human character traits. That is why the comparatively recent discovery of other planets within our solar system does not invalidate astrological observations. It is not that we are under the influence of the planets, but rather that the universe mirrors the ebb and flow of our energy patterns. As the Swiss psychologist Carl Jung observed after a lengthy study of the subject, 'Everything that takes place at a particular moment of time has a quality associated with that moment.'

Astrology has survived through the centuries not because of its accuracy to predict our fortunes, but because it is the practical expression of the ageless wisdom as summed up in the ancient maxim 'As above, so below'.

Some of the greatest intellects in the past were convinced that there was much of value in studying astrology, among these were Plato, Plotinus, St Thomas Aquinas, Johann Kepler, Goethe, Ralph Waldo Emerson and Jung. Jung was in the habit of drawing up his patient's

horoscopes in the belief that these would reveal hidden aspects of their personality and go some way towards explaining their impulses and thought processes. Kepler, one of the founders of modern astronomy, began as a sceptic, as did many of astrology's most ardent supporters, but was forced to conclude, 'A most unfailing experience...has instructed and compelled my unwilling belief.'

Personal astrology

As with other methods of divination conviction is largely a matter of personal experience, although the statistical evidence in favour of astrology is quite considerable. In the

Left: Although astrology has no proven scientific basis, its practise has been widespread since Babylonian times (Celestial map 1661).

1970s Professor Alan Smithers of Manchester University lent credibility to the astrologer's claims by analysing data on over 2 million people taken from the British Population Census to prove that there was a definite bias towards certain career choices depending on an individual's birth date. For example, electricians were invariably born in the winter, architects in the spring, secretaries in the summer and miners in the autumn.

Before Professor Smithers published his report he turned his raw data over to the British Astrological Association and asked them to calculate which sun signs should correspond with the various professions. To his astonishment they correctly predicted his findings. In addition, the members suggested more specific statistical connections. For example, they calculated that nurses were more likely to be born under six particular sun signs and trade union officials under one or more of the remaining signs. When the professor compared the graphs of over 35,000 nurses and union officials the correlations were found to be uncannily accurate.

Positive proof

A few years later the sceptics had more 'evidence' to consider when the French statistician Michel Gauquelin found a correlation between the rise and culmination of the moon in relation to the planets and a successful career choice. It was Gauquelin's conclusion that planetary movements had a link to personality traits which in turn dictated an individual's choice of career. And if they chose their career according to their instincts they were invariably successful.

However, contrary to the impression given by the astrological forecasts in the national press there is more to astrology than simply identifying the Sun sign. Of equal importance are the Moon and the Ascendant, the planet which predominated at the hour of birth. If the Ascendant is the same as the Sun sign then the characteristics of that sign will be intensified. But if the Sun sign and the Ascendant signify opposing characteristics then they could complement each other or in extreme cases cause conflict and indecision.

In 1976, 186 scientists including 19 Nobel Prize-winners, took the extraordinary step of endorsing a manifesto titled Objections to Astrology in which they called for publishers to cease promoting what they saw as superstitious nonsense. Their action had been precipitated by a popular revival of the ancient art which they saw as a threat to the status of orthodox science. However, they did not get support and their protests were ignored.

One of the most neglected aspects of astrology, but one which is now growing in popularity, is the use of birth charts to identify causes of illness and to suggest appropriate and effective cures.

The principle behind this approach is that illness is invariably a manifestation of psychological disease and as a birth chart is, in essence, a map of the psyche it should be possible to predict what illnesses an individual is prone to and what psychological tendencies will trigger them. The patient can them be treated holistically to restore their sense of balance and wellbeing.

A do-it-yourself health diagnosis

Ideally, it is best to consult a qualified astrological therapist to have a general health reading, but if this is not possible you can make an approximate diagnosis for yourself using the following guidelines.

The first thing to do is, of course, to identify your sun sign from the following list:

Birthdate astrological sign
December 22–January 19
Capricorn
Jan 20–February 18
Aquarius
Feb 19–March 20
Pisces
March 21–April 19
Aries
April 20–May 20
Taurus
May 21–June 21
Gemini
June 22–July 22
Cancer
July 23–August 22
Leo
August 23–September 22
Virgo
September 23–October 23
Libra
October 24–November 21
Scorpio
November 22–December 21
Sagittarius

Next you will need to know which of the four triplicities, or elements, you belong to by finding your sun sign in the following list:

Fire signs:
Aries, Leo and Sagittarius
Air signs:
Gemini, Libra and Aquarius
Water signs:
Cancer, Scorpio and Pisces.
Earth signs:
Taurus, Virgo and Capricorn

The elements provide a general indicator of the psychological characteristics of each sign and the pattern of illness with which they are traditionally associated.

Fire types tend to be energetic individuals whose recklessness can result in accidents or a strain of the vital organs. They are also thought to be prone to fevers which are expressions of an excess of vital energy that has not been channelled into something constructive.

Air types are traditionally seen as being rather volatile and more easily upset than the other signs. At the extreme they might be provoked into inducing psychosomatic illnesses to avoid difficulties and what they see as being the unreasonable demands of others.

Water types personify the emotions and have a tendency to be anxious and over-sensitive. As a result they are often prey to stomach troubles, generative problems and hormonal imbalance.

Earth types are grounded, practical people but they can also be prey to illnesses associated with inertia such as circulation problems, stiffness of the joints, skin disorders and some digestive complaints.

These tendencies are strikingly similar to the chart of traditional correspondences in common use by physicians during the Middle Ages and the Renaissance in which the signs of the zodiac were aligned with various parts of the body:

Aries with the head
Taurus with the neck and throat
Gemini with the arms, hands, lungs and nerves
Cancer with the breasts and stomach
Leo with the heart
Virgo with the intestines
Libra with the kidneys and lower back
Scorpio with the genitals
Sagittarius with the hips and liver
Capricorn with the skin and skeletal system
Aquarius with the circulatory system
Pisces with the feet and hormones.

It is necessary, however, to stress that these descriptions indicate a tendency to particular problems and are not to taken as a predictive diagnosis. Other factors, such as infection and stress, can cause or aggravate ill-health regardless of personality type, although the effect of the illness and the severity of the symptoms can differ considerably according to personality type. A bullish Taurian, for example, might refuse to be deterred by a heavy cold, whereas a sensitive Scorpio may well submit to self-pity, using it as an excuse not to do anything which it thinks will have little chance of success.

Palmistry

You don't have to be psychic to practise palmistry, but it does seem to help. A reasonably accurate reading can be obtained simply by studying the principal lines and mounts in the palm and then looking for their significance in a book on palmistry, but what is not commonly known is that the lines can alter with age. Chinese palmistry places considerable emphasis on studying these subtle signs, but the Western forms concentrate mainly on the more obvious features. So, a degree of psychic sensitivity will help to give a more detailed and informed reading. The best palmists are said to be those who do not look at the palm at all, but instead read its energy patterns by tracing the lines and mounts with their fingers.

Ancient traditions

Palmistry is popularly associated with wandering gypsies and fairground fortune tellers, but it is believed to have originated in India more than 4500 years ago where it was practised as one facet of a vast repertoire of esoteric skills known as the Samudrik Shastra ('the ocean of knowledge'). From there it is believed to have spread to the Far East, Egypt and ancient Greece where it found enthusiastic advocates among the philosophers Pythagoras and Aristotle. But the early Church condemned the practise as heresy and its

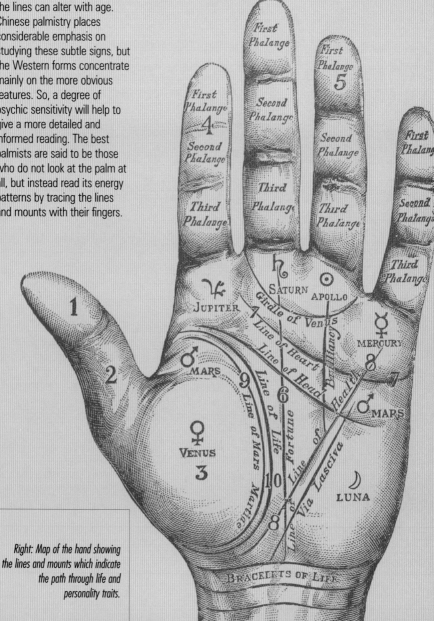

Right: Map of the hand showing the lines and mounts which indicate the path through life and personality traits.

Left: Contrary to popular belief, the features of the hand are not fixed, but alter with age and experience.

There are seven mounds on each palm one roughly positioned at the base of each finger, one at the thumb and two on the plain opposite the base of the thumb (see illustration opposite).

The Mount of Jupiter A well developed mount indicates an uncompromising character while a small mount suggests indecision.

The Mount of Saturn This signifies our attitude to life's challenges. A flat mound suggests that the sitter has had comparatively few problems to overcome or that they do not see these as problems, while a prominent mound indicates a person who enjoys pitting their intellect or resourcefulness against a problem. In contrast, an overdeveloped mound indicates that problems are invariably viewed as being insurmountable.

The Mount of The Sun This mount signifies creativity with a flat mount suggesting undeveloped or undervalued talents.

The Mount of Mercury This mount corresponds to the communication of ideas with a flat mount suggesting difficulty in expressing ideas and a lack of self-confidence, while an over prominent feature indicates the potential for self-deception.

secrets became entrusted to the gypsies.

Although palmistry is commonly thought of as a means of telling a person's fortune, a branch of the art known as chirognomy studies the pigment and texture of the hand as an indicator of health as well as personality.

What happens in a consultation

A good palmist will be able to tell a great deal about your character and your relationship with other people just from observing the way you present your hand for the reading. If, for example, you give your hand with the fingers curled inwards it indicates that you are protective and willing to compromise to accommodate other people, particularly your family.

Traditionally, the left hand is considered to be the template for the talents and tendencies which are present at birth and is called the inactive hand,

while the right hand is the blank on which we inscribe our progress to date and is therefore known as the active hand. In left-handed people the principles and names are reversed.

In recent years palmistry has sought to assimilate aspects of modern psychology in an effort to shake off its earlier associations with fortune- telling. For this reason many practitioners now attribute the creative and intuitive qualities to the left hand and the more logical and practical impulses to the right in accordance with what is known about the functions of the left and right hand sides of the brain.

The meanings of the lines and mounts

In simple terms the lines are seen as the paths through life indicating events in the past, present and future, while the mounts, or contours, indicate the character traits.

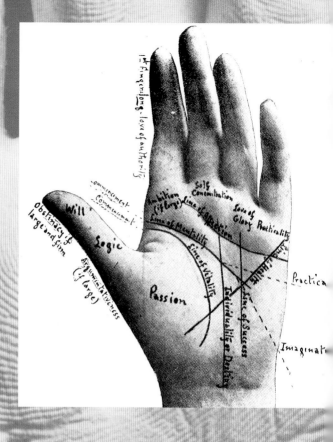

The Mount of Mars Mars in this context corresponds to energy with an undeveloped mount indicating a fear of confrontation and an overdeveloped mount suggesting an inclination to dominate a situation.

This mount is linked to a feature known as the Plain of Mars which extends in an inverted triangle from the mount to the wrist. The upper portion, known as the Quadrangle, determines the influence of the mount and relates to our attitude to other people. A broad quadrangle indicates a need to be forthright and open, a large quadrangle can suggest bluntness and a degree of insensitivity while a narrow area can suggest secrecy.

The lower portion of the plain of Mars, which is known as the Triangle, moderates the influence of the mount balancing action with the intellect. A large Triangle indicates that the individual considers all the options before they act, a long shape suggests that they act out of consideration for others, while a tapered Triangle suggests they feel inhibited in expressing themselves for fear of what other people might think.

The Mount of the Moon The moon has traditionally been symbolic of the intuition and imagination. An over-developed mount suggests unrealistic expectations of life, while an under-developed mount can be suggestive of a serious and practical personality.

The Mount of Venus As its name implies this is the mount corresponding to the emotions.

A well-developed mount indicates a mature and balanced personality who is not prey to their passions, an undeveloped mount could indicate a reluctance for someone to trust their emotions, and an over-developed mount suggests emotional turbulence.

The Life Line A long Life Line does not necessarily signify a long lifetime, but rather stable and steady progress. However, it could be argued that an 'easy' life might not contribute much to a person's character or life experience and that it might be of more value to have an erratic Life Line which indicates challenges and change.

It would also be a mistake to regard this line as a predestined pattern foretelling of future events. Instead it should be seen as a line on which life's experience will be written. We can alter the course of our lives at will and deepen the line by the energy we put into living.

The Heart Line This is the line of the emotions. A well defined line indicates sensitivity, a coarse line suggests a passionate nature, while a faint line is suggestive of a sentimental personality.

Left: a long life line does not necessarily indicate a long life, but rather a smooth passage with few challenges.

The Head Line This is the line of the intellect. A strong line is indicative of a logical mind rather than a measure of intelligence, but of equal importance is the line's relationship to the surrounding mounts. If it begins at the mount of Jupiter it is suggestive of a wilful or determined character, whereas if it begins from the plain of Mars it suggests a degree of intolerance.

The Line of Saturn
Sometimes called the Line of Fate this line indicates how we react to events and adversity. If it is long and well defined it shows a tendency to accept problems as learning experiences. However, an indistinct line indicates that the sitter is easily discouraged by unexpected difficulties and when these arise they have a tendency to think that they give confirmation that life is unfair.

The Line of the Sun
Sometimes referred to as the Line of Fortune this line indicates the chances of success in one's chosen career with a strong line indicating determination and tenacity and a faint line suggesting a tendency to trust to Fate rather than one's own resources.

The Line of Mercury It was once thought that this line foretold of ill-health, but it is now considered indicative of our current state of health (in the active hand) and our likely physical reaction to stress and inner conflict (on the passive hand). A well defined line suggests an inner calm, a thin line indicates a nervous nature and a short line can suggest a difficulty in expressing the emotions.

The Intuition Line This is the line of the psychic senses which appears on our hand as awareness and intuitive powers increases.

Miscellaneous marks In addition to the main features there are many more minor marks that can appear on either hand as character develops and experience etches something new into the palm. Dots, for example, are believed to indicate wealth while square shapes can indicate the need to establish firm foundations before embarking on a new project or relationship. The significance of these subtle signs will be determined by the influence of the nearest mount and line.

A question of balance
There is more to palmistry than simply knowing the meaning of the lines, marks and mounts. If an accurate, overall picture of the sitter's personality and potential is to be drawn, then the relationship between these features and the transient lines which link them have to be taken into account. For example, when the three major lines of Heart, Head and Life are of unequal length and strength it could be that the person finds it difficult to make a decision because their emotions prevent them from making a commitment.

Conversely, if the Head Line is prominent, but the Life Line is weak the individual might be frustrated by not having enough energy to see their plans through to a conclusion. If the reading makes them aware of these traits then they can be realistic in their ambitions and not over-stretch themselves.

It is also important to remember that these features are not fixed, but can alter with age and experience as talents are either developed, or go unrecognized and ambitions are either realized, or never come to fruition.

Crystal gazing

Scrying, the art of foretelling the future by gazing into a crystal ball or indeed any reflective surface, has an unfortunate association with gypsy fortune-tellers and fairground charlatans, and yet it was once a required discipline in the esoteric arts of the ancients.

Babylonian seers and Chinese magicians used bowls of coloured water, the ancient Greeks stared into the still waters of moonlit lakes and mirrors and the Egyptians practised staring into a pool of black ink held in the palm of their hand – a practice that is still popular in Arab countries today. Nostradamus, probably the most celebrated seer of them all, whose cryptic prophecies have fascinated generations, used a similar method to one adopted by the priestesses of the Greek Oracle at Didyma, namely meditating upon a reflective brass bowl filled with water.

What medium to use

The medium used seems unimportant as long as it serves to induce a state of light trance in the scryer. This dissociation of consciousness is an aim of most meditation and relaxation techniques, but by using a 'crystal' as a focus for the inner vision a specific psychic faculty is awoken.

It is significant that the Buddhists refer to quartz crystal, the purest crystal and the ideal medium for crystal balls, as 'visible nothingness', for it is in the mind's eye that the images appear and not in the crystal, which of course possesses no supernatural properties of its own. However, the image can sometimes appear to be in the crystal because to induce the trance the scryer has to soften their gaze and look through it, just as anyone has to look beyond the sitter when reading an aura.

Interpreting the visions

Scrying in any medium is simple and unlike the tarot, the runes or palmistry, it does not require any occult knowledge. However, it will demand a considerable amount of patience as it can be weeks before anything is 'seen'. As in any form of psychic work it is a question of increasing one's awareness of the subtler levels of consciousness and not simply making a wish for paranormal powers.

The images are interpreted according to where they appear in the medium. It is thought that whatever appears to the left reflects reality, the day-to-day activities of the scryer, or the client if they have one, while those to the right are to be seen as symbolic and will require intuitive interpretation and a basic knowledge of symbolism. The pictures to front and back indicate the immediate future and the remote past respectively.

How to do it You do not need a crystal ball to practise scrying, or even the less expensive glass balls which are now widely available. A bowl of ink or even a large glass of water can be used.

Choose a time and a place where you can be sure of being undisturbed. Then place the bowl or glass on a plain surface or tablecloth, preferably black to eliminate any reflections.

Dim the lights or sit with a single candle and relax into a meditative state. Do not try to see anything but let the images arise of their own accord.

At first you may see nothing, but eventually the surface of the medium will become obscured by clouds. When they part the ball may appear to have turned black and you may have the sensation of gazing into a void. If you feel uncomfortable at this point you could ask that whatever you are to see is revealed for your highest good and the highest good of all concerned and that your understanding of the images is not distorted by self-interest.

But before you begin: a word of warning. Scrying is not suitable for those of a nervous disposition or who are taking strong medication of any kind because it facilitates 'uncensored' communications from the unconscious mind which could be disturbing for an unbalanced personality. There are no accompanying booklets with a crystal ball to help you interpret the images. Visions simply appear as in a dream and if you have no occult training or understanding of symbolism you may find these upsetting, or be tempted to give them a significance that they do not merit.

Main picture: Scrying, as seen in this painting by Burne-Jones, is not concerned exclusively with foretelling the future, but with developing a sensitivity to subtle levels of awareness.

I Ching – the book of changes

The central principle of Chinese philosophy is that life is a series of cyclical changes and that our response to these determines both our happiness and our development. If we view these changes as opportunities for growth then we can ride them like a wave, but if we try to hold back the tide of change, we are certain to be overwhelmed. It is this philosophy which is embodied in the I Ching, an ancient oracle which professes to divine the current state of yin and yang (negative and positive forces) in any given situation and then suggest the most fortuitous course of action.

The origin of the I Ching

The system is believed to have originated in the 12th century BC when a provincial noble, known to history only as Wen, was thrown into prison by the Emperor who feared that he might become a rival in a future struggle for power. The resourceful Wen did not despair, but occupied himself with devising definitive meanings for a traditional divinatory system derived from tortoise shells. By the time of his release he had revised the original system of three line patterns to arrive at a more comprehensive oracle of 64 hexagrams. To each of these he attributed his inspired interpretations and philosophical commentaries upon life which were later added to by his son.

Seven hundred years later the elderly Confucius expanded upon these and in so doing lent the system a respectability that was to fascinate modern western intellectuals such as the rationalist philosopher and mathematician Gottfried Leibnitz and the psychoanalyst Carl Jung. It is said that the last wish of Confucius was to be given another 50 years to study the system, while Jung saw it as confirmation of his theory of syncronicity, or 'meaningful coincidences' which help forge a link between the conscious and unconscious mind.

How it works

Consulting the oracle is simply a case of casting three coins a total of six times and recording the number of 'heads' and 'tails' that are thrown. Heads are recorded as Yang lines and tails as Ying. If, for example, after the first throw there are two heads and one tail, an unbroken Yang line is recorded. If after a second throw there are two tails to one head, then a Ying line would be noted. The hexagrams are built from bottom to top with the first throw giving the bottom line and the last throw the top line to complete the pattern.

There are 64 possible permutations each of which has a symbolic significance to be found in the Book of Changes. The individual lines are also capable of interpretation, but only when the influence of the neighbouring lines indicates that they may be about to change into their opposites. This is where the ancient philosophical concept of cyclical change becomes relevant to the reading as a change of line will create a new hexagram whose significance will qualify the meaning of the first. In this way the I Ching is capable of providing 4,000 individual answers.

Dreams and divination

There is much anecdotal evidence to support the oracle's uncanny reputation for accuracy. In Man and His Symbols Jung records the

Left: The decision to attack the US naval base at Pearl Harbour in December 1941 was taken after the Japanese High Command had consulted the I Ching.

experience of a patient who was disturbed by the unusual imagery of his dreams. The patient, an intellectual introvert, was persuaded to consult the oracle and was startled to discover that it made several key references to both his dreams and his psychological condition, specifically his tendency for fantasy and self-deception. Shortly afterwards he had a dream in which he saw a helmet and sword floating in the air and had no idea what it could mean. This time he consulted the Book of Changes without casting the coins and to his amazement he opened it at a page describing the 30th hexagram, Li, which includes helmets and swords in its symbolism.

This 'meaningful coincidence', as Jung would call it, had a profound effect on the patient who had been denying his unconscious impulses as irrational and irrelevant to his intellectual interests. Once the possibility of other realms of awareness were revealed to him through his experience with the I Ching he was able to reconcile both his intellectual pride and his intuitive impulses and the cure was complete.

Main picture: The I Ching is capable of providing individual answers to every conceivable question we can devise.

CHAPTER 4

SOUL SEARCHING

With the decline of interest in organized religion the less dogmatic and seemingly more enlightened philosophies of the East have become increasingly attractive to the Western mind. In particular Buddhism and Zen appear to offer direct experience of the spiritual states and place the emphasis on personal growth rather than adherence to a specific doctrine or deity in order to manifest the divine within.

But millions of ordinary people, regardless of belief, and sometimes in defiance of their convictions, experience mystical and altered states of consciousness such as out-of-body experiences, psychic sensitivity and, less rarely than we might believe, encounters with angelic entities. 'Reality' is an illusion sustained by the limited perception of our physical senses. Once the boundary is breached and we experience this greater reality our lives can never be the same again.

Main picture: Virgil and Dante contemplate the damned in hell, which the esoteric tradition teaches is a creation of the distressed mind.

Buddhism – the search for nirvana

When Buddhists prostrate themselves before the image of the Buddha they are not worshipping Siddharta Gautama, the founder of the religion, but are acknowledging their own Buddha nature. Buddhism is not a religion of blind faith and adherence to a specific doctrine, but rather a philosophy which offers guidance for the seeker to find the divine within themselves. The term 'Buddha' means 'Awakened One' and refers to the state of enlightenment which Siddharta attained and sustained through meditation. It is said that we all have the potential to achieve a state of supreme understanding, known as nirvana, by following the middle way; a path between indulgence and asceticism.

The four noble truths

The middle way is built upon what Siddharta called the four noble truths. These seek to identify the causes of all human unhappiness and show the means by which we can transcend this to find peace of mind.

The first noble truth is that all life is suffering, by which the Buddha meant that no matter what wealth or success we gain it will be undermined by a feeling of restless discontent and a lack of fulfilment, rather than physical pain or emotional turmoil.

The second noble truth is that this suffering is a symptom that springs from being separated from our divine source and with the dissatisfaction that comes from building our lives on transient values and an illusion of life that we call reality.

The third noble truth is that our craving for the vanities of the material world can be mastered and that in doing so we can free ourselves of further suffering.

The fourth noble truth is that the path to nirvana is open to all and can be attained through the mastery of eight disciplines known collectively as the eightfold path.

Above and left: Buddhist monks practise meditation as a control discipline in an effort to attain peace of mind and a sense of detachment.

The eightfold path

The first stage to enlightenment is called Right Understanding, and refers to an understanding of the teachings of the Buddha known as the dharma. In Buddhism faith itself is not a virtue, each individual is responsible for their own spiritual development and so must come to their own understanding of the teachings. The second stage is Right Thought, which requires all those who follow the path to do so with the highest

intention and not so that they can feel superior or self-righteous.

The third stage is Right Speech, which reminds followers to honour the truth and to regard speech as sacred. Words spoken in anger or those which deny the divinity of others can be as destructive as violent actions.

The fourth stage is Right Action, which requires those who follow the path to observe five commandments: Do not kill, do not steal, do not indulge in promiscuity, do not lie, and do not take any form of intoxicant.

The fifth stage, Right Livelihood, requires the Buddhist to practise the precepts of right behaviour whilst earning a living and to resist enriching themselves at the expense of other people.

The sixth stage is Right Effort, which encourages the qualities of self-discipline and devotion.

The seventh stage is Right Mindfulness, which teaches the importance of living in the present moment.

The eighth and final stage is Right Concentration, which aims to still the mind while remaining fully focused so that every experience is valued and not thought of as routine. For in Buddhism life is an expression of the divine. It is only our need to sustain our illusions which prevent us from becoming aware of the greater reality.

The first two stages are considered to be the steps to wisdom, the next three stages constitute the Buddhist moral code while the last three find expression in the practise of meditation.

Through the practise of meditation and mindful behaviour Buddhists can attain peace of mind, greater self-awareness, improved health and the potential for enlightenment within one lifetime.

It is this promise of peace of mind and inner wisdom that has made Buddhism an attractive alternative to many Westerners who have become disillusioned or frustrated by what they see as the demands and empty rituals of orthodox religion.

Buddhism –
the middle way

Our task is to strike a balance, to find a middle way, to learn not to overstretch ourselves with extraneous activities and preoccupations, but to simplify our lives more and more. The key to finding a happy balance in modern lives is simplicity.' (Sogyal Rinpoche)

The Buddhist tradition teaches that spiritual truth and the path to real and lasting happiness is not an abstract concept entangled in a profound philosophy, but is simple common sense.

The Buddhist leader, the Dalai Lama, has said: 'There is no need for temples; no need for complicated philosophy. Our own brain, our own heart is our temple; my philosophy is kindness.'

Cultivating compassion is a principle practice of Buddhist belief, but it involves more than mere sympathy or recognition of another person's needs. It is a determination to do whatever is practical to alleviate

suffering. Contrary to the popular image of Buddhist monks as being reclusive, unworldly ascetics, they instead believe that only through our actions can we realize our Buddha nature. But in being compassionate the Buddhist does not recognize pain as a reality, but as a symptom of the illusion. With compassion must come detachment; described as being in the world but not of it.

Our Buddha nature
One does not become a Buddha, because we already have a Buddha nature as our innermost essence, although we may not be aware of it. Instead we realize our true nature through a process that involves the peeling away of layers of illusion. As the avatar Sai Baba has observed: 'I am God, you are God. The only difference is that I know it and you do not.' An avatar is an

enlightened soul who reincarnates periodically to raise the consciousness of humanity.

We first have to accept that we are, in a sense, addicted to suffering because it reinforces our sense of having a unique and separate identity. This distorted reflection of our true self is what is commonly called the ego and it is this shadow that is afraid of death and so clings to the illusions of life in order to make itself significant. Once we accept this duality we can begin to manifest, or realize the Buddha within.

How to reach enlightenment
The journey to enlightenment, to peace of mind, is inward and takes the form of meditation and mindfulness. For the Buddhist meditation is not something to be mastered, but a state of mind that we should slip into as effortlessly as does the person who relaxes at the

Right: The journey to enlightenment begins in silent contemplation in which the inner voice of the true nature can be heard.

end of a satisfying day's work and simply lets go of all thoughts.

In the West we tend to think that we have to struggle to attain peace of mind and that when we find it we have to grasp it firmly in case it slips through our fingers. But we can no more possess peace of mind than we can possess anything else in this world of illusion and impermanence.

Sogyal Rinpoche, one of the modern Tibetan Buddhist masters, advises us to perceive meditation in the following terms: 'In meditation, be at ease, be as natural and spacious as possible. Slip quietly out of the noose of your habitual anxious self, release all grasping, and relax into your true nature...When you meditate there should be no effort to control and no attempt to be peaceful. Don't be overly solemn or feel that you are taking part in some special ritual; let go even of the idea that you are meditating. Let your body remain as it is and your breath as you find it.'

Rinpoche likens the mind to a vessel of muddy water which when stilled will become clear as the silt sinks to the bottom. In this state of 'calm abiding' all negativity will be dispelled, aggression dissolved and confusion evaporated.

Many beginners learn meditation in the hope of having ecstatic visions or insights that will dictate how they should live their lives and they are disappointed when they experience only silence. But it is in the silence that the real transformation takes place.

However, it is not enough to practise meditation, mindfulness, detachment and compassion unless we can maintain this awareness in daily life. And that is something that no one can be taught. They have to come to that realization themselves.

The wisdom of Zen

In the Zen tradition there is a story that seeks to express the relationship between humanity and its creator and in doing so also explains the apparent paradox at the heart of the philosophy itself.

It is told that the Empress Wu could not understand how it was possible for the diversity of life to share a common source, or Oneness, and so she asked the Zen master Fa-tsang for an explanation. He responded by arranging for eight large mirrors to be placed in a room of the palace, one at each of the eight points of the compass with another on the ceiling and one on the floor. He then suspended a candle from the ceiling in the centre of the room and lit it as the Empress entered. To her delight the room was illuminated with reflected light.

'Your majesty,' said Fa-tsang, 'this is the One and the many.'

Zen Buddhism is a philosophy that defies definition. It is said that no one, not even the Zen masters themselves, are able to convey its meaning in words, for to explain it is to explain it away. It is a religion without creed, doctrine or scriptures because these would only preserve ideas and not the reality which Zen seeks to reveal.

The meaning of Zen

The true meaning of Zen is as elusive as love, or life itself. It can only be experienced. That is why the Zen masters resort to the use of what appear to be illogical riddles, or koans, in order to illustrate that true understanding is beyond the rational mind. These have been described as being like fingers pointing at the moon and we are urged not to confuse the indicator with the object which it is indicating.

A good example of the way in which a Zen master will challenge a pupil's perception can be discerned in this typical exchange:

Pupil: *'Master, I have nothing'*.

Master: *'Then throw it away'*.

The idea of possessing anything is an anathema to the Zen buddhist who considers time, space and form to be an illusion. For the pupil to declare that they have nothing implies that they still cling to the idea that they can have something to give away.

Sometimes, the master will not even respond with words but might hit the pupil with a stick! This is to rebuke the pupil for thinking in terms of abstractions. If the master had given a wordy explanation the pupil would have analysed it and treasured the idea rather than the truth behind it.

Zen philosophy

The essence of the Zen philosophy is summed up in the story of the master who was about to address his students when a bird began to sing. The master said nothing but listened to the bird and the students too fell silent. When the bird had finished its song the master announced that his address had been given and went on his way.

Although such antics may frustrate the rational Western mind they have a serious point which is that life is a series of fleeting moments which we should live rather than spend in discussing its possible meaning. The Zen master sees no value in giving his students

Below: A Zen monk contemplates
the temple garden which reflects the
minimalist philosophy.

ideas about life, but rather
gives them life itself. Zen
confounds the logical western
mind because it rebukes us for
thinking that life is about
something, rather than simply a
moment of being.

In a continuation of the
Buddhist belief that envisages
life as a continuing unfoldment
and our resistance to change
as a living death, Zen asks us
to listen to the music of life as
the master and pupils listened
to the songbird and not try to
preserve it. The real meaning of
life according to Zen is in the
act of singing and not in the
notes themselves. If we
dissected the music that the
bird had made we would be no
nearer to understanding the
elusive magic of music, only
the mathematical relationship
between the notes. And as any
musician or music lover will
know, the secret of music is in
making the notes live again,
and not just playing
mechanically through the
score.

The Tibetan Book of Living and Dying

Since its publication in 1992, The Tibetan Book of Living and Dying by Sogyal Rinpoche has become a primary source of spiritual guidance for those seeking inspiration from the ageless wisdom of the East. In reinterpreting the teachings of Tibetan Buddhism for the modern seeker, the Tibetan born writer and teacher encourages us to go beyond our fear and denial of death to reveal the real meaning of life.

It is Rinpoche's belief that the source of much of our ill-health and unhappiness originates from the pressures that we put ourselves under as we rush to cram everything into a single lifetime. If we could accept that death is only a transition between lives and that each life is to be regarded as a learning experience, he believes that we could transform our fears and frustrations into understanding, awareness and fulfilment. In short, if we knew what lay behind death then we might also understand what lies behind life.

Our fear and ignorance of death and the afterlife is not only lessening our enjoyment of life, it also blinds us to the consequences of our own actions. Rinpoche argues that if we understood that in a future life we will reap what we sow in this current incarnation, then we would not be so blasé about how we treat each other or contribute to the slow poisoning of the planet.

The Bardos

At the heart of Tibetan Buddhism is the belief that life and death are inseparable and that life is effectively a preparation for death. The transitional realities that we experience between lives, known in the Tibetan tradition as the Bardos, are actually occurring continually during both states, not just in death

Main picture: A funeral procession in Nepal. In Tibetan Buddhism death is considered the crowning moment of our lives.

Right: The Wheel of Life, from which only we can free ourselves.

as is commonly believed. At these junctures the opportunity for enlightenment or liberation are heightened and we then have the possibility to break free from the cycle of death and rebirth.

The fact that most of us are not consciously aware of these opportunities is due to fear which desensitizes us; fear that we will lose our unique identity if we surrender to the Divine within, as we must inevitably do. But in resisting and insisting that the ego is all that we are, we are denying our true nature. We are afraid to let go of who we think we are in order to discover who we really are. But if we do not accept that we are more than the persona we present to the world then we are living an illusion and, in Rinpoche's words, 'we will remain imprisoned in the very aspect of ourselves that has to die'.

This suggests that we do not give sufficient significance to the lessons and opportunities of life and that consequently we view death with a greater significance than it merits. The ultimate truth at the heart of the Buddhist philosophy is that life and death exist only in the mind, they are not states of being, only of perception.

Life preparation

Most of us live our lives like the pigeon of the old Tibetan proverb which spends all night fussing over the making of its nest only to find that dawn comes before it has finished. The dawn seems a good metaphor for death, for in Buddhism it is regarded as the crowning moment of a person's life, provided that they have spent their life in preparation for it. This preparation involves the focusing of the mind through meditation and contemplation because it is thought that it is our mind, our consciousness, which survives. If we have not learned to master our minds then when death comes we will be prey to its restless fancies and fears and so create our own heaven and hell.

The ultimate paradox and the central truth at the core of the Tibetan teachings is that the only thing that we can be certain of is the impermanence of life and that if we cling to these illusions for fear of change, then only suffering can result. We fear to reflect on death because we consider it morbid, and yet only by reflecting on the impermanence of all things, can we hope to awaken to the truth which is that the only thing we truly possess and can experience is the present moment.

Out-of-body experiences

One day in 1828 the captain of a cargo ship was accosted by a crewman who had rushed on deck in a panic to report that he had seen a ghost. The seamen, first mate Robert Bruce, described seeing a stranger writing on a slate in the captain's cabin. The stranger appeared solid enough but he had such a look of foreboding on his face that Bruce had fled from the scene and did not want to return. When the captain followed Bruce below they found the cabin empty but for a message scrawled on the captain's slate which read, 'Steer to the Nor'west'.

The captain's first thought was that the crew were playing a practical joke, but the look on his first mate's face convinced him otherwise. He had Bruce and every other member of the crew write the same message on the reverse of the slate, but none of them matched the handwriting of the original message. A search of the ship failed to discover any stowaways and the captain was inclined to change his course if only to solve the mystery and put his own mind at rest.

Three hours after giving the order to steer to the Northwest he raised his telescope to his eye and saw in the distance a ship that was crushed against an iceberg. It was only a matter of minutes before it would sink beneath the waves.

He ordered the lifeboats to be lowered and all the survivors were rescued. But as the third lifeboat was unloading its shivering occupants, seamen Robert Bruce was startled to see that one of the men was the 'ghost' that he had interrupted in the captain's cabin earlier that day.

Ghostly encounters
When the stranger had been fed and rested Bruce and the captain visited him in his berth and asked him to write the mysterious message on the underside of the slate. Incredibly, the writing was identical, but the stranger was just as dumbfounded by the story as were his hosts.

It was only after some thought that he recalled a strange dream that he had earlier that day after falling asleep from exhaustion. He had dreamt that he was aboard a ship that was coming to their rescue and woke to reassure his fellow survivors that they would be saved. Moreover, he described the ship that was on its way to rescue them and was correct in every detail as the captain of the wrecked ship was later to confirm.

This story, originally published in Footfalls on the Boundary of Another World in 1860 by Robert Dale Owen, is one of the most remarkable incidents of astral projection or out-of-body experiences on record, but it is not unique. Statistical research suggests that as many as one person in five has a clear recollection of having had an out-of-body experience.

It is thought that we all experience the phenomenon from time to time during sleep, sickness or when suffering from severe stress, but that we tend to dismiss the episode as a dream or mental aberration because our rational mind is simply incapable of understanding how consciousness can be separated from the physical body. There can be few people who do not recall the sensation of floating or flying during their dreams, or of falling just prior to waking up (which is believed to be the return of the astral body to the physical shell), but upon waking such a concept strikes many rational people as simply beyond belief.

Spirit world

However, the idea that we each have a soul that survives the death of our physical body is fundamental to all the major religions and many of the primary philosophical systems. No less than 57 contemporary cultures adhere to the belief in some form of a 'spirit double', while many esoteric traditions envisage a series of subtle bodies, one within the other, each composed of increasingly finer matter to enable it to survive on the appropriate inner plane.

The phenomenon first came to public attention in 1929 with the publication of a book entitled The Projection Of The Astral Body which had been co-authored by psychical researcher Hereward Carrington and Sylvan Muldoon, an American who claimed to have had numerous experiences of etheric projection over the years. Muldoon described how his frequent illnesses had facilitated the process by weakening the connection between the astral and physical body. And he described the process in detail, including the fact that the astral was connected to the physical shell by an infinitely elastic silver cord which enabled him to travel wherever he wished. He even recommended various techniques which he had found to be effective in inducing the experience.

Main picture: We all have out-of-body experiences but few people are aware of their significance.

Near-death experiences

Astral projection, or out-of-body experiences (see pages 94–95) are often confused with the phenomenon known as the near-death experience, but they differ in one significant detail. In the former the astral body lingers in the physical world, but is able to float through solid objects because it is composed of finer matter. In many cases the astral traveller visits friends and relatives who are usually unaware of their ghostly guests, but who are subsequently able to confirm the accuracy of their observations.

Involuntary projection most commonly occurs during surgery when the patient is under a general anaesthetic. Dr Russell MacRobert of the Lennox Hill Hospital in New York City recorded the case of a clergyman who was able to give a detailed description of the operation including the conversations that took place between the staff and their relative positions during the proceedings, all of which was subsequently confirmed by the surgeon.

The clergyman had left his body as the anaesthetic took effect and he then followed the surgeon out of the operating theatre to retrieve a special surgical instrument that he had forgotten to bring with him. He

watched with mild amusement as the flustered surgeon returned to the theatre to put on a fresh gown and gloves at which point his astral self told the surgeon off for swearing in front of a man of the cloth!

What happens in an NDE?

In the near-death experience the astral body becomes conscious of other dimensions, including a heavenly paradise, and then returns to the physical body with a detailed and objective recollection of all that it has seen and sensed.

In 1937, the eminent professor of anatomy, Sir Auckland Geddes, recounted details of a near-death experience before a gathering of the Royal Medical Society of Edinburgh which hints at the worlds beyond our own. Geddes claimed that the experience was that of a physician who wished to remain anonymous, but it was probably that of Geddes himself who feared ridicule by the medical establishment.

The 'physician' had been feeling ill for some time and one morning awoke with the realization that his condition was critical. He resigned himself to his fate and at that moment sensed his consciousness separating into two distinct aspects; the first concerned with his mental awareness and the second with his physical body. The latter subsequently disintegrated leaving the former to exist independently outside of the body which it could observe with detached indifference. The astral body was evidently clairvoyant as it

Above: Many of those who have returned from the near-death state have described being drawn up through a tunnel of light.

could zoom in on scenes anywhere in the country to which its attention was directed for in this dimension space had no meaning, only time. 'Now' was the equivalent to 'here' in the three-dimensional world of matter.

The physician came to the realization that existence was a series of interpenetrating dimensions and that our brains were merely end-organs, the physical receptacles of a 'psychic stream' which permeated all the dimensions.

When we tuned our minds to a specific frequency we could become aware of these other realities just as a radio can tune to certain wavelengths.

The fourth dimension

As he fine-tuned his sensitivity to the fourth dimension he became aware of the varied, multi-coloured auras surrounding his neighbours in the physical world which suggests that while our physical bodies are confined to the three-dimensional world of matter our astral body, or spirit double exists in the fourth dimension and that possibly our soul exists in the fifth. When we raise our awareness from the mundane to these finer dimensions that is when we become receptive to insights, inspiration and may also have a sense of the unity of existence.

Before the physician had a chance for further exploration he saw a friend enter his room and telephone for a doctor. At the same time he saw the doctor receive the call and the frantic efforts made to save his life.

Like many people who experience NDE's the physician was reluctant to return to the confines of the physical world. 'I was drawn back, and I was intensely annoyed because I was so interested and was just beginning to understand where I was and what I was seeing.'

Although Geddes continued to deny that the experience had been his own he assured his colleagues that it was to be taken as fact and added that it had helped him to accept, 'the idea of a psychic continuum, spread out in time like a plasmic net.'

Below: The astral etheric body is said to be a spirit double of our physical form.

The number of individuals who claim to have ventured beyond the astral plane into the heavenly realms is considerable. They are also remarkably consistent in detail. So much so that they make a most convincing case for life after death.

There have been numerable case studies of the phenomenon since Dr Raymond Moody published his pioneering collection, Life After Life, in 1975 in which he compared 150 separate incidents. These identified a number of common elements including a profound feeling of peace at the moment of death, the effortless detachment of the 'spirit' from the physical body and a journey down a long tunnel to a pastoral landscape where friends and relatives were there to welcome the 'deceased'. All who made it this far described an overwhelming sense of peace and the feeling that they had 'come home'.

The young Indian girl

When a young Indian girl, known only as Durdana, was resuscitated by her father, a doctor, after having been declared clinically 'dead' she described finding herself in a verdant garden through which flowed four streams. These were coloured white, brown, blue and green. There was no sun in the sky, but the almost translucent flowers and fruit trees shone with their own luminescence.

The toddler was greeted by her grandfather who had died some years before and by his mother. But there was also another older woman who the child did not recognize but described as looking like her own mother.

Durdana heard her father calling for her to come back at which point her grandfather said that they would have to ask God if she could return to the world below. The child later described God as a formless blue light from which a voice asked if she wanted to go back. She replied that she had to go because her father was calling and with that she returned to life.

A couple of curious details convinced her parents that the experience had not been a

Above: The astral body of an adept, as envisaged by C.W. Leadbeater, a leading figure in the Theosophical Society.

Left: One of the many early photographs claiming to be of an astral body (1911).

dream brought on by her illness. Firstly, Durdana described returning 'from the stars' to wake on her father's bed. She did indeed wake up on her father's bed but in her delirious state she could not have known it was his. She had only ever been allowed to sleep or play in her own bed or her mother's. The only way she could have known it was her father's bed was if she had indeed seen herself lying there as she returned to her body. The second curious feature was that she later identified her great grandmother from a collection of photographs in her uncle's house. Her parents did not possess any pictures of the old lady who had died before Durdana was born.

There is also a fascinating footnote to the little girl's story. In 1980, twelve year's after Durdana's experience, she appeared on British television with her father to discuss the possibility of life after death. To illustrate her story Durdana showed some of the pictures she had painted of the heavenly garden and the following day one of Durdana's father's patients – a Mrs Goldsmith –contacted the family because she had visited the very same place during a Near-Death-Experience and was able to describe other details which Durdana had not put into her paintings!

A figure of light

The uncanny parallels between these experiences and the traditional images of heaven are striking, but cannot be explained away as the result of cultural conditioning. Although a number of people have described meeting a figure of light who emanated an aura of irresistible bliss and compassion, it is only after they return to waking consciousness that they identify this benign being in terms of their own beliefs.

Although one might expect such experiences to be highly subjective these images were shared by those with different religious beliefs and even by individuals who had no belief in an afterlife at all.

The return to the physical body was often unwelcome with many wishing to remain in the light, and others reluctantly submitting to the 'pull' of the physical body or the nagging of their own conscience reminding them of their responsibilities on earth.

As one doctor remarked after successfully resuscitating a patient who later claimed to have had an NDE, 'I have worked with people many times to get them to accept their death; but this was the first time I have ever had to get someone to accept life'.

Once they have returned to life everyone who has had an NDE, without exception, views life from a new perspective. They tend to be less intense and more compassionate. They embrace life with renewed vigour and say they have nothing to fear from death.

The medical establishment has tended to dismiss their testimony as hallucinations resulting from the effects of medication or lack of oxygen to the brain, however hallucinations are by nature random and senseless. Neither does this theory explain how the brain can produce hallucinations when the ECG traces are flat, registering no activity at all in the brain.

Most curiously of all, perhaps, is the fact that in many cases patients, including young children, have been able to accurately describe the resuscitation procedures and recall the conversations of the medical staff who were absent by the time they recovered.

Angels and demons

In the early 1960s a young Dutch girl and a friend were cycling among the sand dunes at Wassenaar on a beautiful sunny day when they were suddenly and inexplicably overcome with an intense feeling of fear. In the next moment a man appeared with his arms outstretched as if barring the way and told them that it was forbidden for them to go any further. He was dressed in light blue overalls and his extremely handsome face radiated a great love and compassion.

The girls' fear immediately subsided and they heeded his words and turned back the way they had come, cycling all the way home in silence without asking each other what the man had been doing there or why they had obeyed him without question. The following day they discovered that a young girl had been raped and murdered by a psychopath just beyond the spot where they had been stopped and at the same time that they had been overcome with fear. They were in no doubt that they had been saved from being victims by an angel in human form.

There are thousands of similar stories which have been reported by ordinary people in recent times, suggesting that angelic encounters are not the exclusive preserve of biblical prophets, saints or mystics. In fact, some of the greatest minds of the civilised world have claimed to have been enlightened by angelic beings, these include: the poets Dante Alighieri, John Milton, Johann Wolfgang von Goethe and William Blake and the intellectual visionaries Emanuel Swedenborg and Rudolf Steiner.

Do angels exist?

The overwhelming number of sightings and the credibility of the witnesses make a convincing case for the existence of angels, while the recent proliferation of angel books and contact courses, which promise to put anyone in touch with these benign celestial beings, prove that our fascination with angels persists into the digital age.

Angels have stubbornly refused all attempts to confine them to one specific faith, but have spread their protective wings to touch every culture and creed across the globe. They have appeared to believers and non-believers alike, to those who doubt the existence of God and to the faithful. They assume all manner of forms, often contrary to what the witness would have expected, but the one consistent factor in each and every case, is that they always come in a spirit of love. Some materialize to rescue someone from physical danger, while others appear as luminous apparitions bringing words of comfort and an overwhelming sense of serenity to the person concerned.

Angelic encounters

These differ from other supernatural experiences in three important respects:

The first is that angels invariably appear at times of crisis to bring reassurance to the sufferer that the difficulty is only temporary and that ultimately, all will be well.

The second distinguishing feature is that their presence is accompanied by an inexpressible aura of the miraculous which defies any subsequent attempt at a rational explanation.

And the third characteristic is that it is such an intense and sacred experience, even for those people who previously had no interest in spiritual matters, that they are profoundly affected by it for the rest of their lives. It is not a question of them finding religion, but rather a new meaning to their lives and a suspicion that the physical world is only a dim reflection of a greater reality.

According to the psychics and 'sensitives' who claim to be able to channel communications from these celestial intelligences, the veil which separates our world from the angelics is becoming more transparent year upon year as we move towards the next phase in our evolution. This phase will involve a raising of consciousness so that people will gradually become aware of the invisible realms and their inhabitants.

You do not have to be religious to appeal for help from the angels, nor do you have to subscribe to a specific belief system. You just need the belief which says that as an innately divine being you have the right to ask for assistance from those who serve the universal life force and the right to expect their assistance.

Main picture: The visionary artist and poet William Blake claimed to have drawn angels 'from life' and to be inspired by them throughout his life.

Above: Contemporary descriptions of angelic encounters are in stark contrast to the traditional beautific image.

Guides and
angels

The following exercise is designed to enable you make contact with each of the angels who are said to govern the seven chakras, the subtle energy centres in the human body. You can use this exercise to revitalize yourself if you feel drained of energy, to balance and centre yourself if you are in need of deep relaxation, or to open communications with the angels.

Tuning in

Make yourself comfortable in a straight backed chair, close your eyes and begin to focus on your breathing.

When you feel sufficiently relaxed say to yourself, 'I am going to count from one to ten and when I reach ten I will be in a very deep state of relaxation and heightened awareness in which I will be receptive to the love, light and healing energy of my angelic guides'.

Then visualize the number one and the colour red. Red corresponds to the colour of physical energy and the vibrational frequency personified by the angel Gabriel whose Hebrew name translates as 'Strength in God'. Absorb red into every cell of your being and feel the life force revitalizing and reinvigorating you from within.

Next, see the number two in your mind's eye and the colour orange. Orange is the colour of the emotions and corresponds to the vibrational frequency of the angel Uriel whose name means 'The Light of God'.

Then visualize the number three and the colour yellow which is symbolic of the sun. Saturate yourself in yellow, draw upon its healing power and as you do so become aware of the living presence of the angel Raphael whose name translates as 'The Healing Power of God'.

Now visualize the number four and the colour green, the colour of harmony and of nature, a symbol of the border between the natural and spiritual realms. Visualize the lush green lawns and hedges of a celestial garden the domain of the angel Michael whose name translates as 'Like Unto God'.

Next visualize the number five and the colour purple, a colour associated with intuition. Psychic sensitivity is ruled by the angel Zadkiel whose name means 'Righteousness of God' but is more accurately translated as the quality of integrity.

Next visualize the number six and the colour violet, the

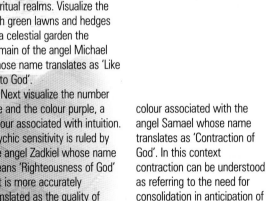

Above: A traditional image of the Archangels by Botticini (1446-97).

colour associated with the angel Samael whose name translates as 'Contraction of God'. In this context contraction can be understood as referring to the need for consolidation in anticipation of change and new developments.

Now visualize the number seven and the colour blue, symbol of unconditional love. Blue is the colour corresponding to vibrational frequency of the Guardian Angel who we reach through surrender of the self or ego.

Next visualize number eight and the colour gold, which corresponds to the frequency of vibration personified by the angel Raziel. He is the personification of earthly power and celestial glory whose name translates as 'Secret of God'.

Now visualize the number nine and the colour silver

personified by Zaphkiel, the angel of Contemplation, whose name translates as 'Wisdom of God'.

Finally, visualize the number ten and the colour white, the purest of colours from which all other colours come. White is personified by the archangel Metatron whose name means the 'Spirit of the Presence' and whose role it is to oversee the ever unfolding evolution of existence. Absorb yourself in white. Draw a circle of white light around you, below your feet and above your head to create a sacred space in which to communicate with the angels.

Now is the moment to ask for their guidance or assistance on various areas in your life.

When you feel that you have completed your contact with the angels return to waking consciousness gradually by counting slowly down from ten to one. Became aware of your breathing once again, the weight of your body, and when you are ready open your eyes.

For a further explanation of chakra points and their associated positions in the body see pages 154–157.

Psychic abilities under scrutiny

Everyone possesses a degree of psychic sensitivity, although they may dismiss it as intuition or an inexplicable 'feeling' they have about someone. But while some people choose to develop this ability through specific forms of meditation and work under the guidance of psychic groups, others are content to let it remain dormant. And yet, who has not experienced 'dèja vu', that nebulous sense of having had an experience before the actual event occurs. Or the feeling that someone they haven't seen or heard from for sometime was about to telephone or visit shortly before they did so?

Paranormal phenomena

Scientific research has proven conclusively the case for the existence of paranormal phenomena in 'ordinary' individuals and yet, the scientific establishment remains stubbornly sceptical. In the 1930s Dr J B Rhine, the father of experimental parapsychology, conducted an exhaustive series of experiments over eight years into psychokinesis ('mind over matter') using students from Duke University (North Carolina) as his subjects. He proved beyond all possible doubt that anyone can influence the fall of dice if they make a determined effort when their level of interest is highest and they are fresh and alert.

In subsequent sessions the students' success rate declined sharply with each successive test which suggests that our ability to manipulate matter is dependent upon the degree of 'will' power we can summon and that this declines when we become bored. It seems likely that the majority of humans remain unaware of their own innate abilities simply because they are content to live routine, predictable lives which dulls their psychic sensitivity.

Scientific analysis

Since Rhine published his results a number of celebrated psychics have readily submitted to scientific scrutiny, one of the best known being the American artist Ingo Swann. In the 1970s Swann experimented with plants. He bought the unhealthiest looking specimen of *Dracaena massangeana* that he could find, took it to his New York office and began to cultivate a psychic relationship with it to the amusement of his colleagues. They became less cynical, however, when Swann revealed that the plant had been asking him for a penny for its pot which one of the staff realized must be a reference to

Above: An early demonstration of telekinesis involving table levitation.

Left: A subject attempts to predict randomly generated numbers.

Convincing the physicists

But this most impressive performance was still to come. At Stanford Research Institute in California, physicists Harold Puthoff and Arthur Hebard devised a formidable test which required Swann to influence the magnetic field in a magnetometer, a highly sensitive instrument for measuring magnetic fields. To prevent any influence from an external source, the core of the magnetometer was surrounded by four separate shields and encased in an eight-ton iron vault set in concrete beneath the laboratory floor. Swann's psychic probing instantly doubled the frequency of the waves traced by the instrument's recorder and then, to the astonishment of the sceptical scientists, he stopped the magnetic activity entirely. The lines of the recorder went flat. After 45 seconds, Swann declared that he could not 'hold it' any longer and the magnetic activity resumed as indicated by the undulating patterns drawn by the recorder.

For his final display Swann drew the shocked scientists a sketch of the interior of the magnetometer including features that he could not possibly have known were there. He had passed the ultimate test and the physicists declared themselves convinced.

the mineral copper oxide. A few cents were duly inserted in the soil and some hours later the drooping plant made a full recovery.

In a subsequent experiment Swann attempted to influence the health of a plant belonging to Cleve Backster, a former CIA interrogations specialist whose office was in another district of the city. Backster had wired up a philodendron to a machine that measures electrical resistance so that he could study the extra-sensory perception (ESP) capabilities of plants. Whenever Swann imagined himself pouring acid on its leaves the plant's electrical resistance responded with wild erratic waveforms as if registering panic. But in time the responses decreased as if the plant had learned that the threats were unfounded.

Swann later submitted to a rigorous series of tests for the American Society for Psychical Research during which he repeatedly identified objects

and geometrical shapes that had been placed out of sight on a platform above his head. In an extension to this experiment Swann agreed to demonstrate an ability known as 'remote viewing' where he would project his consciousness to a group of coordinates randomly chosen by the research team. In 100 separate tests he was able to supply detailed descriptions for 43 of the locations which proved to be unerringly accurate, and 32 descriptions which were correct in many respects.

On one occasion he 'returned' with a detailed description of a island in the Indian ocean of which the researchers were unaware. They insisted that there could be nothing there but water. Undeterred Swann made a sketch of key features including a landing field, jetty, boats and a lighthouse which were subsequently verified in every respect after the island had finally been located.

In search of 'faculty X'

We tend to think of psychic powers as a 'gift' bestowed upon a small number of people by a benevolent universal being, and in doing so we reinforce our suspicion that life is a lottery to be enjoyed or endured depending upon what fate has thrown our way. By the same token we imagine that enlightenment is beyond the experience of ordinary mortals; something to be striven for by an ascetic who must renounce the world and retire to a spiritual retreat to live the life of a religious recluse.

And so, with no personal experience of higher consciousness and no aspiration to seek such an experience, nor hope of having one, the majority of humanity sinks into a mundane mindset until a crisis shocks them into a realization of their own mortality and stimulates a search for a meaning to life.

A greater reality

In contrast, the experience and the insights shared by those who claim to have glimpsed a greater reality suggests that we all have the potential to replace 'the robot' with our 'real self' and to maintain that state of heightened-awareness,

but that many of us choose not to do so. We prefer to keep our blinkers on, to keep our vast mental supercomputer on 'stand-by', because we fear change, although without change there can be no growth, only stagnation.

A cybernetician once remarked that if we wanted to build a computer as complex as the human brain it would have to be the size of the moon and yet, most of us live at a very low level of awareness, fantasizing about possibilities that we fear to pursue in case we fail, worrying about what the future might hold, repeating our mistakes and reliving our regrets until we drain our vitality.

We seek stimulation in peak experiences such as sex, food, fast cars and even stress, all of which give us a sense of purpose and confirm that we are indeed alive. But perhaps

the most extraordinary aspect of human nature is our willingness to deny our divine potential and to settle for a state of awareness which is the equivalent of sleep-walking in a world of infinite interest and variety.

Expanding consciousness

The writer Colin Wilson concluded his exhaustive survey of supernatural phenomena, The Occult, with the comment that the enemy of life is not death but forgetfulness, by which he meant that we allow our true selves to be lost in the anonymity of the material world. We may be spiritual giants in essence, but within the limitations of the physical body we perceive the panorama of life through the equivalent of a tiny crack in a fence. Consequently, we develop a narrowing of our consciousness and eventually succumb to a form of inertia, or mental laziness, in which we lose interest in finding out who we really are and what we are capable of.

Wilson predicts that the next step in our evolution will be to develop an expansion of consciousness, from the microscopic to the telescopic. He argues that we already possess this capacity which is the basis of all occult experience, and which he calls 'faculty X', but that we are simply not aware of it. Our fascination with art, literature and music stems from their ability to induce a degree of

'faculty X' by stimulating the imagination and through that mechanism to allow us to experience an almost mystical detachment in which we temporarily lose our everyday selves. But faculty X is not only the means by which we can 'grasp the reality' of the past and of other places, but also of the present moment. It is the equivalent of what the Buddhists call 'mindfulness' and without which we are merely cruising through our days on automatic pilot.

What we perceive to be reality is in fact only symbolic of a greater reality which we all glimpse from time to time without appreciating the significance of the experience. The English writer and academic C.S. Lewis had such an experience while reading a

favourite book associated with happy memories of his own childhood. But it was not a desire to return to his childhood that prompted him to return to the book, it was 'the idea of Autumn' and the intense desire to reawaken the total experience of being alive to its meaning. 'It was something quite different from ordinary life and even from ordinary pleasure; something, as they would say now, "in another dimension".'

That sense of meaning is what we all unconsciously long for and occasionally experience through the symbols of the greater reality.

Below: Psychic powers are not a gift to an élite group, but a degree of awareness beyond the mundane.

Pathworking

Pathworking is the term given to a specific form of visualization exercise in which the practitioner imagines themselves in a certain situation and in doing so projects their mental self, or consciousness, into another dimension. But although pathworking is considered to be a highly subjective experience, in which the imagination is used to bridge the abyss between the conscious and unconscious realms, its effects are real enough. With practise the inner planes can be experienced with full sensory perception and the practitioner can interact with the beings that exist at those levels for the purposes of gaining self-knowledge and greater awareness.

The term is derived from Kabbalistic practise where the various levels of awareness are seen as corresponding to the paths and spheres on the Tree of Life. However, as a form of meditation it is thought to date back to the magical practises of ancient Egypt and possibly even beyond to Sumeria, the first civilization.

Once the jealously guarded secret of esoteric orders and occult secret societies, the technique is now widely practised as an element of psychoanalysis under the name Active Imagination, where it is used to guide the patient into the realms of the unconscious. The essential difference between the esoteric and more clinical forms is that in the former the practitioner is acquainted with their chosen path and the signs and symbols along the way, whereas in analysis they will be led by the therapist.

Using mythical characters

In the esoteric field those who feel an affinity for the Arthurian legends, for example, might practise pathworking using the mythical characters of Arthur, Guinevere, Lancelot and Merlin. Envisaging these archetypes within a guided visualization can help the practitioner to explore, strengthen and integrate those aspects of their own personality. Tarot initiates might use the symbolic images of the individual cards to do the same thing, while Kabbalists would use the Tree of Life as a template, or map, of the invisible realms and envisage the angels of the sephiroth or other archetypal images as personifying the divine attributes at each level.

Initial exercises would be limited to a journey inwards into the psyche before any attempt is made to explore the corresponding levels in the spiritual dimension. However, some practitioners would make no distinction between our inner being and the greater reality of which we are an indivisible element, and would consider pathworking as simply a highly focused method of achieving a potentially enlightening altered state of consciousness.

How it works

When the mind is focused through the will in this way and empowered with the desire to bring about change then we can literally make our dreams come true. That is the basis of every self-help book on the

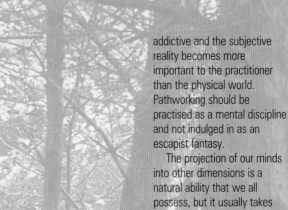

market, although most people will not get the result they seek because there is more to it than simply wishing for what you want. The dream has to be imprinted on the astral plane by sustained and focused thought until it draws matter like iron filings to a magnet to help it materialize in the physical dimension.

By reprogramming the unconscious mind through creative visualization you can, for example, attract new job opportunities or improve a relationship. Bringing about change in the outer world through altering your own state of consciousness is the true meaning of magic, but there is more to magic than exercising willpower. You can attract anything into your life through creative visualizations of this type, but what you make of what you wished for will depend on whether or not you accept the responsibility that comes with it.

When to use pathworking

There is no danger in pathworking unless it becomes addictive and the subjective reality becomes more important to the practitioner than the physical world. Pathworking should be practised as a mental discipline and not indulged in as an escapist fantasy.

The projection of our minds into other dimensions is a natural ability that we all possess, but it usually takes the form of a daydream and as such the potential benefits are lost.

Regular practise will bring sustained growth on a personal level and other practical benefits, such as increased concentration and self discipline.

We all practise pathworking every day of our lives, although we are not conscious of the fact. Whenever we have a journey to make or a task to be accomplished we will imagine the process stage-by-stage to fix the details in our minds and ensure that we have all we need to complete the work. If we are apprehensive about attending a job interview, for example, we will probably visualize ourselves in the situation to psyche ourselves up for the ordeal.

But even if we don't consider ourselves to be particularly imaginative, or the type that is given to daydreaming, we will still periodically practise a form of pathworking whenever we relive past events by recalling pleasant memories. If you doubt the power of pathworking just think back to a particularly pleasant time in your life and let yourself be immersed in the emotions that it arouses.

Pathworking – the tower of illusions

To experience the power of pathworking for yourself work through this guided meditation once a week for six weeks and see how the experience intensifies with practise. The imagery has been chosen to attune you to a specific level of consciousness, but once there allow the details to arise spontaneously and try to resist the temptation to analyse the symbolism until you have returned to the waking state. It is advisable to record the script onto cassette so that your concentration is not interrupted by having to refer back to these notes.

Make yourself comfortable, close your eyes and begin to focus on your breathing. Feel yourself relaxing with every breath. Go deeper into the warm, comfortable darkness of relaxation with every breath.

When you feel sufficiently relaxed visualize yourself standing in the outer courtyard of a temple complex. The floor is comprised of black and white squares symbolising the complementary universal forces which are unified in existence. To either side of you rise two pillars, one of white ivory and the other of black marble symbolising form and force. This is where your inner journey begins.

Before you are three archways leading to the inner courtyards. Each of these entrances is obscured by a heavy black curtain on which is painted a symbol from the tarot trumps. On the curtain to your left is the Wheel Of Fortune which symbolizes the laws of karma, the situations which you create for yourself as the results of your past actions. On the curtain to your right is the image of The Fool, symbol of the eager innocent setting out to explore the world. It also represents the qualities of self-determination and free will. You always have free will to choose your path in pathworking as in life. However, on this occasion you are going to take the middle path, the entrance of which is obscured by a curtain on which is painted the symbol of The World. The World represents discernment, which is said to be the lesson of this life. We constantly have the choice between what we call Good and Evil, those actions and thoughts which manifest our divine nature and those which deny it. This is the place we must leave on our journey back to the source of our being as symbolized by this journey into the inner sanctuary.

Pass through the curtain with the symbol of The World and see yourself on a path leading to a small walled enclosure a few hundred yards straight ahead of you. There are cloisters to either side of you, but no other people to be seen. You enter the garden through a door in the wall and find yourself alone in a garden dedicated to childhood. Let the details arise without any effort on your part. You may find mementoes from your own childhood here. If you do, what memories and emotions do they awaken?

Above: No matter how fanciful the images appear, if they are spontaneous they may be of great significance to you.

When you feel that your visit here is complete for the time being leave by another door, one that you find to the right of the entrance. Walk along this path until you come to a tower. What state of repair is it in? How tall is it? Is it a watch tower, a bell tower or a folly?

Enter and climb the spiral staircase which winds all the way to the top. When you get to the very top what do you find? You notice a curtain in one corner. Drawing it aside you find a full length mirror. How do you appear in the glass? As you confront this image of yourself the sky darkens and the tower is momentarily lit by lightning. The flash reveals a hidden facet

Left: Pathworking often draws on myths and legends as these contain universal archetypes and situations.

of your personality. Is this an aspect that you fear to acknowledge or a quality that you have denied?

Another flash and a roll of thunder shakes the tower to its foundations and you make your way back down the stairs as swiftly as you can.

Retrace your steps to the garden and pass through it noting any changes that might have been made since you were last here. Return through the curtained archway to the outer courtyard and remain there for a few moments considering the implications of what you have seen and experienced.

When you are ready return to waking consciousness by counting slowly down from ten to one. Write down all you have seen while the images remain vivid in your mind.

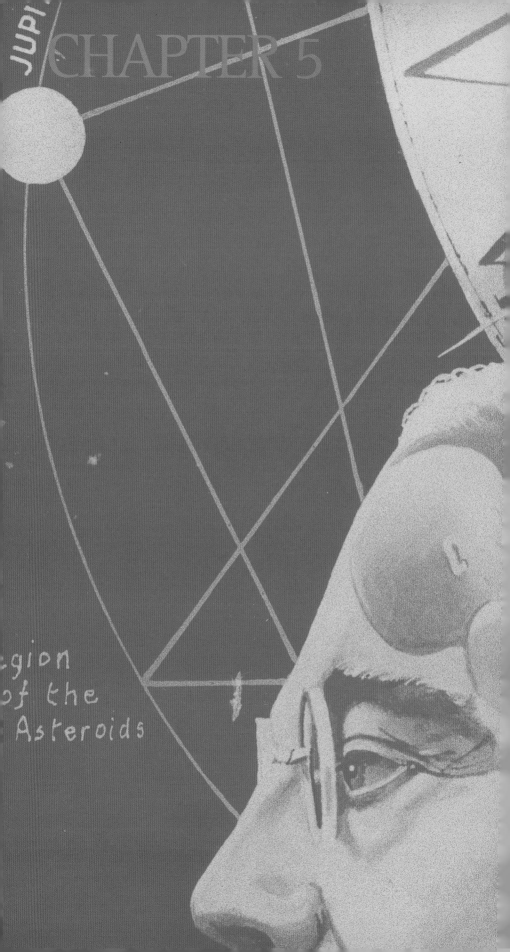

CHAPTER 5

gion
of the
Asteroids

INNER CHILD AND HIGHER SELF

There are currently over 400 different approaches to psychoanalysis with many differing quite radically in their understanding of the human psyche. Some state categorically that we each possess three distinct types of personality which correspond to distinct stages in our development and that these manifest according to stimulus or the needs of the situation. Others contend that we possess a single, multi-faceted personality whose innumerable and diverse aspects are the sum of our experiences and cannot be readily identified. In contrast, the esoteric tradition envisages an eternal struggle between out true self, or immortal soul, and our ego.

Main picture: Science views the brain as the origin of all our impulses and instincts, whereas the estoteric tradition sees it as the physical sense organ, responsible for limiting and censuring a greater reality.

In two minds

One evening in the late 1880s the editor of a Detroit newspaper, Thomas Jay Hudson, an avowed sceptic on the subject of psychic phenomena, attended a seance with a difference. The difference being that this seance had no intention of inviting any spirits. It had been convened by a renowned physiologist called William B. Carpenter who was determined to demonstrate that psychic phenomena are the product of the subjective mind.

Humans, he argued, have two minds – the objective and the subjective. The objective mind deals with mundane, practical matters and the subjective is concerned with memory and intuition.

Hypnotic conversations

To prove his point he put a young college graduate under hypnosis, whom Hudson referred to in his report as 'C', and suggested to him that he had the ability to summon the spirit of the philosopher Socrates. C was sceptical where spirits were concerned, but his subjective mind evidently accepted them as a reality because it had been programmed to see them. Carpenter then encouraged C to engage the spirit of the dead philosopher in conversation and to repeat aloud whatever Socrates said in reply for the benefit of the audience.

Contrary to expectations C held a more than credible 'conversation' with Socrates for more than two hours. In fact, Hudson reported that the intellectual arguments were of such a high calibre that the audience began to believe that C really was in communication with a spirit. Encouraged by this performance Carpenter 'introduced' C to the spirits of more recently deceased philosophers and again the 'discussion' was extremely convincing with C responding with genuine astonishment at some of the spirit's statements. This suggests that the subjective mind – if that indeed was the source of the statements – is a separate entity with its own ideas and is not simply a repository of memories and obsolete information.

Hudson described this session as producing a system of spiritual philosophy 'so clear, so plausible, so perfectly consistent with itself and the known laws of Nature that the company sat spellbound.' Were it to be published Hudson speculated that it would have formed "one of the grandest and most coherent systems of spiritual philosophy ever conceived by the brain of man."

But was it a product of the brain, or could C's subjective mind (what today would be called his unconscious) have linked up with the Collective Unconscious once his rational mind had effectively been 'put

to sleep'? One of the oddest features of the experiment was the marked differences between the language and style of each of the philosophers and C's change in attitude as he responded to each in turn. If they had been merely projections of his subjective mind surely they would still have spoken with his voice and within the limits of his knowledge? Even a talented professional actor would find it difficult to play so many parts with conviction and to ad lib for more than half an hour or so. C had no theatrical training and no script. Moreover, neither memories nor imagination alone could explain how he could sustain a multiple discussion of that quality over several hours and enthral an audience in the process.

The power of hypnotism

Hudson, however, was literally mesmerised by the power of hypnotism and impressed by the retentive capacity of the human memory. For those who still believed that C had been in communication with spirits, he recalled the case of an illiterate young girl who spoke in Latin, Greek and Hebrew while suffering a fever. It transpired that she had once lived in the house of a Protestant pastor who was in the habit of reciting passages aloud to himself in these languages which the girl had evidently absorbed unconsciously.

In a bestseller on the subject, The Law of Psychic Phenomena, Hudson suggested that if we could learn to focus the powers of the subjective mind we could cure ourselves of every physical ailment and

Above: Hypnosis effectively puts
the conscious critical mind to
sleep in order to gain access to
the unconscious.

lead healthier lives. He argued
that a hypnotist can induce a
blister by simply suggesting
that their subject had suffered
a burn and he argued that
stigmata (bleeding wounds)
were induced by saints and
religious zealots by a similar
method.

To prove his theory he
decided to attempt to cure a
relative who was suffering from
nervous convulsions and

rheumatism by merely
programming his own
subjective mind with the
intention every night before he
went to sleep. He informed
two friends of his experiment
so that they could serve as
witnesses, but not the relative
who was living a thousand
miles away at the time.
Hudson began the treatment
on the night of May 15, 1890
and a few months later was

informed by one of the
witnesses who had met the
relative that the health of his
'patient' had shown
considerable improvement from
the middle of May.

Hypnotherapy

Prior to the discovery of ether, it was common practice to use hypnotism to anaesthetize patients against pain. Today, an increasing number of hospitals are reintroducing the technique in the more sophisticated form of hypnotherapy after it was discovered that it can control bleeding and significantly reduce post-operative shock.

The power of hypnosis in reducing the effects of stress, alleviating pain in both acute and chronic conditions, and helping patients to face irrational fears and phobias, is well documented and proven by clinical research. However, it is not so well known that the technique can be used personally if care is taken over the wording of the suggestions to be programmed into the unconscious mind.

The following exercise is particularly effective in reducing stress and dispelling irrational fears and phobias, but it can also be used to establish a more positive outlook on life if it is practised on a regular basis.

How to hypnotise yourself

Before carrying out any self-suggestion procedure, decide what you want to achieve from the session and stick with this one identifiable aim. Do not be tempted to try to sort out all your problems in one go or you risk creating more.

All suggestions directed to your subconscious (unconscious) mind should be:

1 Beneficial and positively phrased. It may sound obvious but an affirmation along the lines of: 'I am going to learn to swim no matter how frightened I might feel' will only reinforce the fear. A more positively phrased suggestion would be: 'I am going to enjoy learning to swim and be healthier, fitter and happier because of it.'

2 Short, direct and unambiguous. For example, 'I will never smoke another cigarette. I do not need them. I do not want them. I am happier and healthier without cigarettes.'

3 Easily memorized. For example, 'I am perfectly acceptable as I am.'

Then write your goal and list your reasons for wanting to achieve it together with the positive effects that you expect from achieving your objectives. Each time you write or repeat

Right: Hypnotherapy can be used to conquer fears and phobias by reprogramming the unconscious mind.

the affirmation, visualize yourself succeeding to reinforce the message on the unconscious.

Getting ready for self-hypnotism Choose a time and a place where you will be undisturbed. Take the phone off the hook or put the answering machine on if you have one. Then make yourself comfortable either by lying on a bed with your arms hanging loosely by your sides, or sitting up straight on a chair with your hands on the arms and your feet flat on the floor.

Focus your attention on something just above eye level (for example, a pattern in the wallpaper, a clock face or a mark on the ceiling), then take

five deep breaths and as you exhale keep repeating the word 'relax'. Sense the tension draining out of you like smoke that has been polluting you from within and is now being expelled to leave you clear and healthy inside.

Now close your eyes and focus on five sounds that you can hear such as the birds singing, the ticking of a clock and your own breath. Then become aware of five things that you can feel at this moment, such as the weight of your own body on the chair or bed, the warmth of your skin, the rise and fall of your chest and the clothes against your body.

Next, scan your body for tension starting at the top of your head. Tense each muscle for a few seconds and then relax it. Now take a deep breath and sigh, exhaling very slowly.

You are now in a deep state of relaxation and can begin the

descent into the unconscious. Visualize yourself at the top of a staircase with ten steps leading down through a bank of clouds to a beautiful garden far below. Run your hand along the side rail as you take the first step...down...feel yourself becoming more relaxed as you take the second step...down. With the third step you are leaving behind your cares and concerns, with step four you lose your critical self, with step five your real self is free, with step six you are entering the clouds,...step seven you are in the clouds and are deeply relaxed, ...step eight you feel very calm, with step nine you emerge from the clouds into the sunlight and the final step ten takes you down onto the velvet lawn.

You are now sufficiently relaxed to impress the chosen suggestions on your unconscious mind. Repeat each suggestion three times, leaving a short pause between each. When you have done this you can either drift into sleep, or count slowly back from ten to one as you climb back up the staircase in your imagination and return to waking consciousness.

The higher self

In recent years complementary health therapists, holistic healers and self-help specialists have begun talking in terms of the need to rediscover our 'inner child' and of learning to love 'the self', as though these are separate personalities that need to be integrated if we are to be complete.

Psychoanalysis acknowledges the existence of multiple personalities in pathological cases and suggests that within even the most balanced individual there are at least three separate aspects of the psyche which are continually shifting in and out of focus. Dr Eric Berne, originator of Transactional Psychology, identifies these as the child, adult and parent – with the child being exuberant and innocent, the adult exhibiting a degree of responsibility and the parent habitually imitating aspects of the individual's own mother or father.

The human psyche

Carl Jung, the Swiss psychologist, believed that the human psyche is more complex than this and cited the case of an American girl who exhibited two quite distinct personalities. In 1811 the girl,

Mary Reynolds, awoke from a prolonged and profound sleep with total amnesia. Over the following weeks she had to re-learn everything that she had once taken for granted including reading and writing. But it was more than simply a case of amnesia. The 'new' Mary was a more lively and fun loving person than the dull and often depressed teenager that her family had known. But the 'new' Mary was not a complete personality either. She proved to be irresponsible and reckless to the extent of endangering her own life on several occasions as might a young child who is oblivious to

the consequences of its own actions.

And then as suddenly as the new personality had come it vanished. Five weeks after losing her memory Mary awoke one morning with all her memories restored and no recollection of the past week's events. Moreover, the old timid, melancholic Mary had returned.

Main picture: The Swiss psychologist Carl Jung believed the human psyche comprises multiple personalities.

Right: The inner child within us all is, according to some psychiatrists, only one of the personalities which makes up the psyche.

Over the course of the next 16 years the two personalities of Mary alternated until they matured into a distinct third personality in middle age. This third Mary was fun loving and lively, but she could also be pragmatic. She had lost both the habit of lapsing into depression and the recklessness. But evidently the third Mary could not have come into being until the other two aspects of her personality had been integrated, albeit through a form of self-imposed 'shock therapy.'

It appears that the old Mary had lapsed into what the analyst William James termed 'a habit of inferiority to her true self' and was shocked out of her stupor by an aspect of herself, Mary 2, that she had once denied. Unfortunately, it was not a gradual assimilation of complementary aspects, but a forced assertion by one facet upon the other. The shock had proved too much and the old Mary had lost her memory as a result.

The case of Mary Reynolds is only one of numerous such cases, some of which involve the apparent manifestation of up to a dozen different personalities.

Different personalities

The Russian mathematician and philosopher Ouspensky envisaged a theoretically limitless hierarchy of personalities which in the normal course of our development we awaken, or 'realize', one by one as we mature. He called these latent stages 'the ladder of selves' with the ultimate, fully integrated, or 'actualized' personality, existing beyond the mental and emotional levels.

This notion of a 'higher' or 'true self', of which we and the other facets of our personality are a part, has been a central concept of the esoteric tradition for centuries. Orthodox religion also hints at the existence of an all-knowing essence at the centre of our being which it calls conscience, or the 'God within'.

It is thought that this more highly developed personality is the source of insight which has provided scientists with the solutions that they were seeking, artists with their inspiration and mystics with the revelations into the true nature of existence.

But only the esoteric tradition actively encourages us to seek to communicate with the essence of our being while we are alive through meditation and exercises such as the one overleaf.

If indeed it is the case that an all-knowing higher self resides like a sleeping giant within each of us, then instead of trying to gain spiritual sustenance we might be better off heeding the advice of the ancient Chinese sages who taught: 'abide at the centre of your being for the more you leave it, the less you learn.'

Communicating with the higher self

The following exercise has been developed using spiritual and psychological principles to establish a line of communication between the conscious and unconscious mind. It is recommended that persons who have a history of mental illness or who are taking strong medication, or are of a highly imaginative and nervous nature should not attempt this exercise.

For this exercise you will need a pen and a large lined notepad or several loose sheets of writing paper.

Choose one of the following affirmations according to your present circumstances or, if there is no specific area of your life that you want to work on at the moment, then be guided by your intuition to make the right choice.

Affirmations:

Wealth and abundance are mine by right and they flow to me in a positive way right now.

I create and sustain harmonious relationships for the highest good of all concerned.

The universe is a limitless reserve of healing energy which revitalises and sustains me.

I abide at the centre of my being which brings me serenity and peace of mind..

I am fulfilling the purpose of my life which is becoming clearer to me everyday.

I am perfectly acceptable as I am.

All that I desire for my highest good I can achieve effortlessly and with the blessing of the universe.

Having chosen the sentence, write it once and then read it silently to yourself. Next empty your mind and allow thoughts to arise spontaneously. Write down whatever comes into your mind without analysing it, even if it sounds like nonsense. Initially, it will seem to make no sense, but after some practice you should succeed in stimulating a stream of consciousness that will eventually develop into a contact with your Higher Self.

Once you have established contact it is important to keep writing until the contact is ended by the Higher Self, although it is possible to interject with questions which should be written down so that you end up with a complete dialogue for later analysis.

Take two minutes in which to write down whatever comes into your mind and then write the same sentence again, listen for two minutes and then write the sentence for a third time. Continue in this way until you have written the chosen sentence a total of 22 times. If you are listening and writing for two minutes between sentences this will mean that the whole exercise will take about 45 minutes. Repeat this once a day for 11 days, then rest for 11 days before choosing another sentence to work on.

Although this exercise can get right to the truth of a difficult situation or increase your general sense of well-being most of us have more than one or two problems that need 'clearing' during our lifetime. For this reason it is recommended that you work through all of the affirmations.

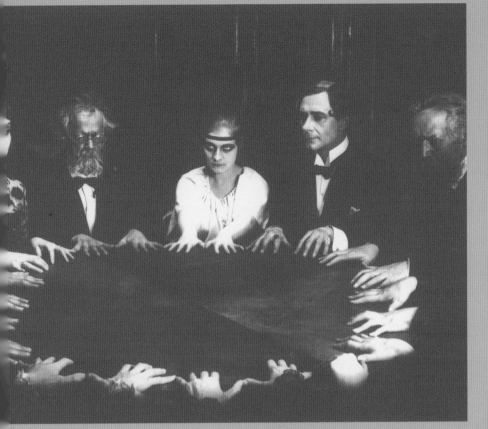

Making contact with your higher self

It is possible that you will 'make contact' with your higher self after just a few days but it is important not to anticipate a result or to try, in the sense of making an effort. The secret of success with an exercise of this nature is to relax and let go, just as in certain forms of meditation.

You will know when you have a genuine communication from your 'spiritual half' when you find yourself writing lines that you did not have time to consciously think about. It will be as if you are taking dictation. This form of 'automatic writing' has nothing to do with possession by spirits, it is purely a means of forging a link between the conscious and unconscious mind and can be stopped at any time without any ill effect or any obligation on your part to continue against your will. Nor is there any suggesting of 'cheating fate' by seeking solutions to your present problems in this way.

Your higher self knows the truth of your present circumstances and is continually trying to communicate with you in the form of intuition, inspiration and dreams, but we are conditioned to dismiss dreams and hunches as products of the imagination. However, the first step in psychic and spiritual development is to learn to regard these subtle impressions as significant. In losing your sense of self to the overself you are only lulling the ego to sleep so that the greater part of you can slip into the driver's seat. You, however, remain in control at all times.

Spirit doubles

In January 1865 Charles Good, a member of the Legislative Council of British Columbia, took his place with other members of the Council for a group photograph. It was a routine sitting in all respects but one – at the very moment that Mr Good was having his photograph taken he was also seen lying in a coma at his home.

Such episodes are not as uncommon as we might imagine. There are so many authenticated cases of bilocation (appearing to be in two places simultaneously), doppelgangers (seeing one's own spirit double) and other related phenomena that they cannot be readily dismissed as just mere illusions. There is the possibility that such apparitions may instead be the result of thought-projection, created by an intensity of desire and animated by the will, as are the thought forms created consciously by Tibetan monks as a part of their mental discipline. Understanding such phenomena may go some way towards explaining the nature of the etheric body and ultimately of consciousness.

Bilocation

One of the most revealing and well documented cases of bilocation occurred in France in the 1840s. Emilie Sagée, a young French schoolmistress, was dismissed from no less than 17 schools in just 16 years because it was said that she had the unsettling habit of appearing in two places at once. Whenever she felt tired and her concentration wandered her double would appear – often standing by her side at the blackboard to the astonishment of the entire class. But as soon as her attention was caught by the chattering schoolgirls the apparition vanished. It was as if her thoughts were wandering in the form which had given them life. On a subsequent occasion, Emilie was adjusting a pupil's dress when a girl

Above: Edgar Allan Poe (1809–49) claimed to have been haunted by his own double, en experience which inspired his tale 'William Wilson' (as shown in this illustration by Harry Clarke).

caught sight of two 'Emilies' staring back at her from the mirror. Not surprisingly the poor girl fainted.

Another time Emilie was walking with a number of her pupils in the school grounds when the girls claimed to be able to see her 'double' through the window of the classroom across the lawn. The girls were initially too frightened to approach the apparition, but eventually a couple plucked up sufficient courage to touch it and described it as feeling like muslin.

Emilie was eventually forced to take early retirement and went to live with her sister-in-law after which the sightings apparently ceased.

Astral projection

Such sightings might be explained as the projection of the astral body, or spirit double, by someone who is literally 'thinking ahead' and willing themselves to be somewhere else. This would explain why the phenomenon occurs most frequently among people who are ill and whose link with the physical body is weakened as a result. Or those like Emilie who do not appear to be sufficiently 'grounded'. But it does not explain the appearance of an individual's double in solid form.

In 1908 two members of the British House of Commons, Sir Carne Rasch and Dr Mark Macdonell, who had been confined to bed by their doctors were seen on separate occasions to take part in critical debates. Dr Macdonell's double even cast his vote, although it is not known if it was sufficient to alter the outcome!

An even rarer form of the spirit double is known as 'the forerunner' from its apparent ability to precede the individual days or even weeks in advance of their physical appearance. In many cases witnesses claimed to have held conversations with the double while the physical person is elsewhere,

unaware of what their 'double' is doing on their behalf.

A good example of the forerunner occurred in 1955 when New York businessman Erkson Gorique travelled to Norway on business for the first time, only to be greeted as an old valued customer by the clerk of his Oslo hotel. Gorique dismissed it as a case of mistaken identity, even though the clerk had called him by name before Gorique had given it. The next day Gorique's

cynicism was utterly confounded when he called on a prospective customer who told him there had been no need for him to make a second trip to Oslo. The Norwegian assured Gorique that they had met and agreed terms some two months earlier!

Below: Dostoyevsky (1822–81), one of many celebrated writers and intellectuals to have experiences the doppelganger phenomenon.

Ouspensky

Everything is alive, there is nothing dead, it is only we who are dead.'

That was the conclusion of Pyotr Demianovitch Ouspensky, the Russian mathematician and mystic whose personal experiences of altered states of consciousness have proven profoundly influential to Western esoteric thought.

Ouspensky's ideas, which are more accurately described as revelations, are thought to have been initially induced by the ingestion of nitrous oxide which, when diluted with oxygen, stimulates heightened perception and a clarity of vision which are in stark contrast to the hallucinogenic effects produced by narcotics.

The American philosopher and psychologist William James described the effects of the gas as stimulating the mystical consciousness 'to an extraordinary degree' and added, 'Depth beyond depth of truth seem revealed to the inhaler...the sense of profound meaning having been there persists; and I know more than one person who is persuaded that in the nitrous oxide trance we have a genuine metaphysical revelation.'

Ouspensky's allusion to death was intended to convey the insight shared by innumerable mystics throughout history, namely that our sensitivity to other levels of reality is dulled by the physical organs of perception. Only by raising our awareness through an effort of will – preferably and most effectively through meditation – can we begin to see through the illusions which form the boundaries of the physical world.

Spiritual awakening

Ouspensky's first experience of this awakening involved the separation of his lower, everyday self from his Higher Self giving him a sense of duality and the realization that everything is interconnected. The boundary between the objective and subjective became blurred as he became a part of what he perceived. As he looked at familiar household objects they suddenly seemed suffused with meaning.

Perceiving the objects with the eyes of his higher self he unravelled an endless chain of events and correspondences which ranged from the materials that it had been fashioned from to the people who had manufactured it. Even inanimate objects were composed of energy to which he could tune in and replay the images and impressions which they retained. But when he returned to normal consciousness Ouspensky found himself with the dilemma faced by many of the visionaries and mystics through the ages, which was the realization that language is incapable of conveying the enormity and significance of such experiences. They are as elusive as our dreams from which we retain little more than a series of impressions and a vague sense of an alternative reality. He was left with a single sentence that he had managed to scribble as the feeling left him: 'A man can go mad from one ash-tray.'

When he did attempt to describe the sensations he found that he was unable to finish a sentence as new ideas overwhelmed him while he was still formulating the next word. It was as if the physical world was grinding along in slow motion while his 'real self' was operating at superhuman speed in a parallel dimension.

The pattern of existence

The knowledge that everything was an indispensable particle in the pattern of existence was intensified whenever he went for a walk in this same state of heightened awareness.

'...there was nothing that remained indifferent for me..there was nothing dead, nothing inanimate...Particularly interesting were the houses and other buildings which I passed, especially the old houses. They were living beings, full of thoughts, feelings, moods and memories. The people who lived in them were their thoughts, feelings, moods. I mean that the people in relation to the 'houses' played approximately the same role as the different 'I's [personas] of our personality play in relation to us. They come and go, sometimes live in us for a long time, sometimes only appear for short moments.'

When observing animals he became aware that they were personifications of an idea, of a form of being and that the nature of the animal found expression in its form. A horse was more than flesh, blood and bones; it was a combination of atoms and consciousness which assumed a form that best expressed its nature.

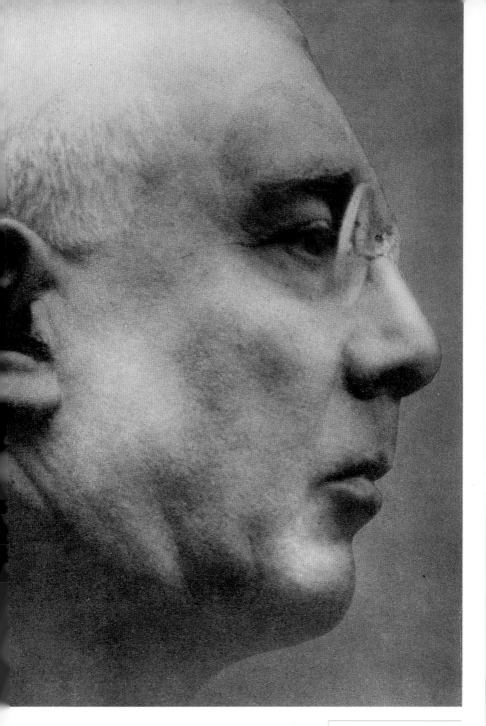

Similarly, human beings are atoms in a greater being.

This sense of the 'rightness of things', of everything conforming to a cosmic pattern and unfolding to a 'will' greater than the individual, is immediately lost on returning to waking consciousness. And each time he came back

Ouspensky experienced the oppressive ordinariness of the physical world: 'The strangest thing in all these experiences was the coming back, the return to the ordinary state, to the state which we call life. This was something very similar to dying or to what I thought dying must be.'

Above: Ouspensky (1878–1947) attained a vision of a greater reality which made physical existence appear lifeless by comparison.

Gurdjieff

'My body seemed to have turned into light. I could not feel its presence in the usual ways. There was no effort, no pain, no weariness, not even any sense of weight.'

The complexity of the human brain and its vast capacity for knowledge is in sharp contrast to our limited understanding of the universe and our place and purpose in it. This apparent paradox has occupied the minds of many of the great thinkers and mystics throughout history, most recently the Russian mystic G. I. Gurdjieff (c.1873–1949), founder of the Institute For The Harmonious Development Of Man.

Gurdjieff was an extraordinary individual, by all accounts. He once discharged himself from hospital and swore to cure himself after sustaining extensive injuries in a horrific car crash from which he was not expected to recover. Within two weeks he was fully recovered and fighting fit, presumably having used a combination of yogic meditation and his own psycho-spiritual exercises. On another occasion it is claimed that he revitalized one of his pupils, who was suffering from nervous exhaustion, by a psychic exchange of energy. The pupil, Fritz Peters, described seeing a violent electric blue light emanating from the mystic which appeared to drain him of life, leaving him slumped and grey in the face. Peters however, was invigorated, claiming that he had never felt better in his life, and that Gurdjieff

recovered his strength within 15 minutes, presumably with some form of meditation.

Everyday consciousness

It was Gurdjieff's belief that we can not hope to evolve until we make the effort to overcome our habitual inertia in which we literally 'forget ourselves' and cease to be active participants in our own lives. To this end he developed a series of demanding physical and psycho-spiritual exercises which aimed to confound 'the robot' that is our everyday consciousness to the extent that it would short-circuit, allowing 'the real self' to take over. This system proved so effective that on one occasion, Gurdjieff's biographer J.G.Bennett, found himself capable of performing superhuman feats, despite suffering from acute dysentery and exhaustion.

Bennett had awoken one morning shaking and consumed with fever. He decided to stay in bed, but found himself rising and dressing automatically as if 'a superior "will"' had assumed command of his body. Despite his exhaustion he joined the morning psycho-spiritual exercise class and soon found himself alone as the other pupils dropped out one by one from fatigue. 'Suddenly, I was filled with an influx of an immense power,' he recalled.

The power of the mind

After the class Bennett felt the need to test the power that had taken him over. He dug over the garden for more than an hour in intense heat at a rate that he could not have sustained in the best of health for more than a few minutes. Again, he felt no sense of effort. Moreover, he experienced a clarity of thought which brought a spiritual awareness of 'the fifth dimension'. He perceived the eternal pattern of everything he looked at including himself.

'I remember saying aloud: Now I see why God hides himself from us. But even now I cannot recall the intuition behind this exclamation.'

Bennett was by now on such a 'high' that he could not rest and so he went for a long walk in the forest marvelling at the 'eternal pattern' that he saw in the intricate tapestry that nature had spread before him. Still in a state of exhilaration and heightened awareness he recalled a lecture by another of Gurdjieff's pupils, the Russian mathematician and mystic Ouspensky, in which the latter stated that we have no control over our emotions. At that moment Bennett willed himself to be astonished and was overwhelmed with the uniqueness of each and every tree in the forest. He then thought of fear and began to shake with terror at imagined horrors in the shadows.

Above: Russian mystic and
spiritual leader Georgei Gurdjieff
(c.1873–1949) who had the power
to transfer vital energy to those who
needed it at will.

With the thought of joy, the
fear instantly evaporated and
he was overcome with elation.
Finally, Bennett thought of love,
and remembers: 'I was
pervaded with such fine shades
of tenderness and compassion
that I saw that I had not the
remotest idea of the depth and
range of love. Love was
everywhere and in everything.'

It soon became too intense
a feeling and he feared that if
he explored the emotion any
further he would cease to
exist. He chose to lose this
new found ability and in the
next instant it left him.

Dreamworking

We each spend almost a third of our lives asleep, 25 years of the average lifetime, and yet most of us are not even curious to know what dreaming is or what its symbolism may signify. To the average person sleep is seen as an unnecessary interruption of life and dreams as the fantasies of a sleeping brain.

In contrast, the psychoanalyst Sigmund Freud called dreams 'the royal road to the unconscious' and placed great significance on their symbolism, most of which he insisted was either sexual in origin, or expressed the dreamer's secret aspirations.

Jung, his former pupil took a wider view. He considered dreams to be a source of spiritual insight from the eternal aspect of our being which he called the 'superior man'. It was his contention that the inner voice of our dreams might be this Higher Self which knows the answers to all the questions we are seeking.

Unfortunately, according to Jung we have lost the capacity to listen to or to interpret the meaning of the symbols with which this superior self conveys ideas and concepts.

Analysis of dreams

In more recent times dreams have become a central source of material in a number of alternative therapies from Gestalt to the more fringe practices of the New Age therapists, but the idea of working with our dreams as a source of insight into our psyche and as a tool for developing self awareness has been practised by many supposedly 'primitive' people for centuries.

For example, The Senoi, who inhabit the Malayan rain forest, hold a daily ritual in which the elders interpret the dreams of both adults and children in the belief that the experiences in the dreamworld have a bearing on waking life. In common with other indigenous tribes from the Native Americans to the Australian Aborigines, the Senoi see the realm of dreams as an inner reflection of the physical world which they visit nightly in their dreambodies, an idea which is strikingly similar to the western esoteric concept of the astral plane.

In the dream world the sleeping person is often forewarned of potential conflict with other members of the tribe and so has a chance to avert a confrontation before it occurs. In this sense dreams are not seen as precognitive but as a communication from the unconscious which has a greater awareness of our situation than does the conscious mind. Dreams also help the Senoi to face their fears and helps them to conquer them. They see the threatening figures of their nightmares as personifying an inner conflict – an idea which has now been adopted by many therapists and counsellors in the West.

Dreams may indeed be dramatizing our desires, but they also reveal what we need to do to be complete. If practised on a regular basis dreamworking exercises will help you to analyse, influence and gain guidance from your dreams so that you can integrate all aspects of your personality and become more complete.

Dreamworking
Here are several simple techniques for improving your dream recall and influencing the content of your dreams.

A dream diary The first step in establishing contact with the unconscious is to take its communications seriously. One of the best ways to do this is to keep a dream diary so that you record the details of your dreams immediately upon waking. This will help to identify your aspirations, anxieties and any underlying patterns of behaviour which may be ensnaring you in the same problematic situation time after time.

It is a frustrating fact that our ability to recall the details of our dreams fades rapidly as we regain waking consciousness so keeping a record will help fix the images for later analysis. But don't be tempted to begin analysing before you have recorded everything that you can remember as the other impressions will sink back into the unconscious while you are considering the significance of the one you think is important.

Main picture: Dreams can be a valuable source of spiritual and psychological insight.

Once you have all the details down on paper try and remember any relevant incidents which may have influenced the imagery of the dream as this might help to explain what may otherwise appear obscure or significant at a later date.

If you suspect that you might be having precognitive dreams the only way to know for certain is to keep a dated and detailed record of them for future verification.

Lucid dreams A lucid dream is one in which the dreamer becomes aware that they are dreaming and then takes control of the dream. The most common experience of this kind ends with the dreamer believing that they can fly and finding the sensation exhilarating. It is thought that such dreams are involuntary out-of-body experiences and

that the sensation of falling which occurs just prior to waking is the astral or dreambody returning to the physical body.

Lucid dreams have been used as a form of therapy for patients who suffer from recurrent nightmares. It is often the case that nightmares, particularly those in which the dreamer is being pursued, are either the result of suppressed memories, or of the denial of an aspect of the dreamer's own personality.

By helping the patient to become conscious that they are only dreaming during the nightmare, and encouraging them to confront their pursuers, therapists have been able to free them of their fears and end the nightmares.

It is quite easy to induce a lucid dream without having to go to a therapist. You simply impress that wish upon your

unconscious just before you go to sleep by repeating the intention to do so in your own words and then reinforcing that desire by deciding in advance upon an incident or symbol whose appearance will trigger the experience.

Gestalt therapy
In Gestalt therapy each character in the dream is seen as a different aspect of the dreamer's own personality. To reintegrate these aspects and make themselves 'whole' again the dreamer is encouraged to either act out each character's part in turn, or imagine what their motivations might have been so that they can gain a new perspective on themselves.

This dynamic branch of psychoanalysis was developed in the 1950s by psychiatrist Fritz Perls who discovered that many of his patients' problems

derived from their failure to become what they thought they ought to be. Perls considered that what was really needed was a form of therapy that would help them to become more themselves by integrating the often contradictory aspects of the personality.

How it is practised Gestalt therapy is usually practised in a group in the presence of a qualified counsellor or therapist where the sharing of dreams, feelings and experiences are considered to be a great help in the 'clearing' process.

However, you do not need to join a group to benefit from gestalt techniques. Instead you could use the contents of a recent dream as the starting point for a meditation in which you visualize yourself taking the part of each of the characters in turn. Once you are in the role, so to speak, you can ask the characters why they behaved the way they did and if they have something specific to reveal to you. You may receive the answers in words or as symbols, or you might find that the dream continues beyond the point where you woke up to reveal its true meaning.

The Dream Journey The Dream Journey is one of a number of alternative therapies which incorporate both modern

psychoanalytic theory and what might be called 'primitive' tribal practises. Such therapies are becoming increasingly popular as analysts and counsellors in the West begin to appreciate the obvious link between ancient 'natural' wisdom and contemporary psychological insights.

The Dream Journey was developed by Californian psychologist Strephon Kaplan-Williams, founder of the Jungian-Senoi Institute, the first dreamwork centre in America. It is based on a combination of Jungian psychology and Senoi shamanic dreamwork and involves developing a dialogue with our dream ego, the image of ourselves which we project into our dreams. It is through integrating, rather than simply analysing the actions of this dream personality that we can wake up to who we really are.

Above: Sigmund Freud (1856–1939), the 'father of psychoanalysis', considered dreams to be the 'royal road to the unconscious'. He is portrayed here in an illustration by Charles B. Slackman.

Kaplan-Williams is convinced that unless we 'actualize' our dreams by regarding them as valid experiences, rather than simply fantasies, we will project our inner conflicts into the external world. Through our dreams he maintains that we can discover our true selves, but to do this we have to become habitually self-reflective and self-aware. If we do not accept the need to change as events arise, he fervently believes that illness will eventually force that need for change upon us.

Left: The author Charles Dickens (1812–70), seen here in a painting by R.W. Buss, found inspiration for his novels in his dreams.

Heal your life

Personal Growth gurus Shakti Gawain and Louise L Hay have become media celebrities in the USA for promoting a positive self-help philosophy which combines the rational approach of the Western mind with the intuitive wisdom of the East. Their practical programmes of creative visualization exercises and affirmations, based on principles developed by the Human Potential Movement, have helped millions of ordinary people to question their limiting and negative beliefs and in effect, learn to love themselves – which is the first significant step on the path to self-transformation and healing.

Louise L Hay

Louise L Hay believes that she was able to free herself from the resentment and regrets of a traumatic childhood which would otherwise have blighted her whole life. Instead, she re-educated herself to think more positively, to reject the habit of self-criticism that she had unconsciously been conditioned to create and to nurture compassion both for those who had abused her and for herself. She developed a course of practical exercises for dissolving her fears and reversing the causes of disease. During this process she claimed to have cured herself of terminal cancer.

In an echo of the Buddhist belief that states that our thoughts create our future Hay sums up her self-help philosophy in the sentence, 'the point of power is always in the present moment'. Her books, lectures and workshops encourage us to question why we hold certain potentially debilitating attitudes, why many of us continually seek the approval of others and why we seek to be loved by others before we have even learnt to accept ourselves as we are.

A typical exercise will involve imagining yourself and your parents as tiny children, all of whom are confused by the world around them and are seeking security and reassurance. A visualization of this kind gives a fresh perspective on those whom we normally only see as adults and it begins the process of rediscovering our 'inner child' without whom we remain isolated in an adult world of our own making, still seeking approval when the only person who we really need to accept unconditionally is ourselves.

Shakti Gawain

Shakti Gawain also preaches a similar approach centring on a technique known as creative visualization which she has helped to popularize. It is a type of meditation in which the power of imagination is used to impress a desire upon the unconscious in the form of an ideal image. This picture of the perfect relationship or occupation is periodically reinforced by positive affirmations which also help to dissolve any resistance that might be preventing us from receiving what is rightfully ours.

Successful creative visualisation depends on three elements; a strong sense of purpose; belief in the goal and the possibility of attaining it; and acceptance of that which we seek. Purpose prompts the question: 'Do I really want this, or could it be a craving for something that I hope will make me happy?' while acceptance relates to those occasions when we expend a lot of physical, mental and emotional energy chasing something because it is elusive. The chase keeps life interesting, but it might not bring us satisfaction or the solution that we seek.

Other techniques include making 'wish lists' which help to clarify what we really want from life, listing our achievements in order to increase confidence and self-worth and scrutinising our self-image as the first step to accepting ourselves as we are.

Gawain identifies a pernicious problem which prevents many people from manifesting what they wish for and what they suspect will bring them real satisfaction. She reveals that many people find difficulty in accepting the best that life has to offer them because they are stifled by a sense of unworthiness. Others are so preoccupied with trying to grab whatever they think they need, in order to do what they want, to make themselves happy, that they shut

themselves off from the source of real happiness. In Gawain's opinion we must first be who we really are, then do what we need to do in order to have what we want.

However, it is not enough to learn to accept ourselves as we are, we also have to accept that the universe is an abundant source of power and spiritual sustenance. If we 'go with the flow' of life instead of trying to vainly impose our Will upon it, it will carry us over the rough spots to the place that we truly belong, which will invariably be even more wonderful than we could have imagined for ourselves.

Above: Personal growth guru Louise L. Hay believes that much of our ill-health and unhappiness comes from negative conditioning in childhood.

Creative visualization exercise

The following original exercise is based on a central concept common to the new generation of popular, self-styled, spiritual psychotherapists led by Shakti Gawain and Louise L Hay. It seeks to stimulate the creation of an inner sanctuary to which you can retire whenever you require a break from the world and at the same time will facilitate visual contact with your inner guide.

Sanctuary of the higher self

Begin by focusing on your breathing. Once relaxed, visualize yourself with your family and friends gathered at the coast by the water's edge waiting to depart on a journey. You are to make a sea crossing on your own, while they will each make their own journeys by land. You will all meet again at your shared destination, a country whose distant shoreline you can just make out as a blur on the horizon.

After you say your farewells and watch them depart leaving you on the shoreline, how do you feel about the prospect of the voyage? Are you excited or apprehensive?

You survey your own boat. What size and type is it? It could be any size from a small rowing boat to a giant ocean liner. Take whichever image comes spontaneously to your mind. Do not try to alter or analyse it now. What condition is it in? Is it large enough to have any crew aboard and if so, what are they like?

It is now evening and you set sail with only minimal provisions and an offering for your own higher self, or inner guide, whose sanctuary you will visit on an island en route. What gift do you bring for it?

For the first part of the voyage the sea is calm, but soon the sun sets, the moon is partly obscured by gathering storm clouds and so when you look to the horizon you can no longer see your destination. As the storm winds gather force the boat is tossed from side to side in the swell and you ask your higher self or guide for guidance to a safe harbour. At that moment the storm abates, the moon appears from behind the clouds and you find yourself approaching the island sanctuary that you have been seeking.

You moor the boat and taking the offering, make your way inland to a secluded sanctuary. It might be a walled garden, a simple shrine or a temple. Again, accept whatever image comes spontaneously to mind. If it is a structure of some sort is it simple or elaborate? Is it well maintained? If there is a garden is it formal or informal? Is it over-run with weeds or is it being looked after?

Take your time to enjoy the atmosphere, the sense of serenity and wellbeing.

When you are ready, place your offering to one side and ask your guide to appear and accompany you on a tour through your sanctuary. As you walk together contemplate how he or she has guided you through life and protected you from your own ego and lack of experience. Know that even when you committed your most foolish and selfish actions he or she did not judge you, but gently guided you and inspired you to see your errors in the light of valuable experience. From now on, if you wish, he will make his presence felt in less subtle ways, but you need to actively seek his counsel by listening for your inner voice.

Now thank your guide and return to the boat. When you climb aboard you notice that a gift has been left for you in return. What is it?

Set off on the second part of your voyage. The sea is mostly calm but there are rough passages which you no longer face with anxiety as your destination can now be seen clearly in the distance. The gift that you have been given also brings the presence of your higher self much closer to assure you that you will never again feel that you are journeying through life alone.

Eventually you enter the harbour at the entrance to this far country where you find your family and friends have gathered to welcome you – each with their own tale to tell. Now gradually become aware of your surroundings once again, sense your body sitting in the chair and focus on your breathing. Count down slowly from ten to one and when you are ready open your eyes.

It is recommended that you do this exercise once a week for three months and then periodically whenever you feel the need for guidance.

CHAPTER 6

HOLISTIC HEALTH

The various complementary therapies described in the following section are currently seen by Western medical science as additional aids in the fight against disease. But they are, in fact, complete systems of healthcare for mind, body and spirit whose effectiveness has been proven over the centuries. In contrast to conventional Western medicine, which is still in its infancy, these systems are not concerned with identifying ailments but instead treat each person individually, that is, holistically, so that the subtle vital energies in the physical and etheric bodies can be brought into harmony and balance. Ailments are generally seen as symptoms of disease in the psyche, which if unheeded eventually manifest in physical problems, rather than as purely physical infections or biological malfunctions. Instead of relying on prescription drugs to attack the symptoms, these treatments instead aim to strengthen the body's own immune system so that it can fight the disease and restore itself to a natural state of wellbeing.

Main picture: Tai chi and the 'soft' martial arts are an integral and essential part of life in China and other Asian countries.

Ayurveda

Ayurveda is Sanskrit for 'the knowledge of life'. It is a holistic health system that mixes science with philosophy which originated in India over 3,000 years ago. Ancient texts such as the Charaka samhita describe the significance of cells within the body many years before the discovery of the microscope brought them to the attention of the medical establishment in the West. Another ancient text, the Susrutha samhita, describes surgical procedures, equipment, stitching techniques and the importance of hygiene.

Ayurvedic philosophy
The principle of Ayurvedic philosophy is preventative medicine rather than a reliance on remedies. Its components include regular exercise, detoxification, a natural, balanced diet, the use of herbs and various techniques to stimulate the circulation of prana (the body's life force) throughout the psycho-biological system. For that reason patients are treated individually according to their constitution and the balance of three vital components known as doshas, which determine our susceptibility to disease, physical features and temperament. The doshas are known by their Sanskrit names vatha, pitha and kapha.

Vatha is the vital energy force which is primarily concerned with the nervous system. Pitha governs the metabolism and digestion – while kapha corresponds to moisture and fat. These three forces, which are often associated with the primary elements of air, fire and water, are in perfect balance when we are born (a state known as prakruthi), but can be adversely affected by emotional and environmental factors as well as poor diet and injury.

According to Ayurvedic philosophy, many of our health problems are caused by the fact that we are attracted to those foods which increase the dominant dosha on the principle that 'like attracts like', and so throw the other elements out of balance. For example, stocky kapha people are drawn to kapha foods which are rich in sugar and fats whereas they should be incorporating more vatha and pitha foods (salty, sour and spicy) into their diet.

Diet affects the digestion, and digestion is the key to good health in the Ayurvedic system as it regulates the elimination of toxins and the assimilation of nutrients.

What happens in a consultation?
The initial session typically lasts for up to an hour and involves the practitioner compiling a personality profile including likes and dislikes, as well as details of your medical history, appetite and lifestyle. A physical examination, which involves looking at the colour and condition of the facial features as well as the tongue, pulse points and hands, will reveal more relevant details.

Treatment
The first stage of treatment is detoxification, as restorative treatments can have no beneficial effect until the body is cleansed of any impurities. Detoxification can be done in a number of ways including a massage with herbal oils, steam baths, oil enemas, herbal enemas, herbal laxatives and herbal inhalation therapy.

The second stage of treatment can include herbal or mineral remedies to restore balance in the doshas. These are often blended by the patient and taken in the form of tea two or three times a day. The final stage involves a lifestyle prescription taking in diet and exercise. A practitioner will often recommend that the patient takes up yoga on a regular basis and refrains from eating the food to which they are instinctively attracted.

How many sessions do I need?
Minor ailments can be cured after two or three visits while chronic conditions can take up to six. Serious ailments may require two or three treatments per week for the initial period, while less serious problems may only involve a single follow-up session a month after the initial diagnosis.

Right: The principal concept of Ayurveda is that illness can be prevented by regular stress-relieving exercises, meditation and a natural, balanced diet.

Which problems can it help?

Whilst cancer and hernias are considered unsuitable for Ayurvedic treatment, virtually all other ailments have been found to respond well, whether they are of a physical, emotional or mental nature. Ayurveda is particularly suitable in the treatment of digestive disorders such as chronic indigestion, constipation, irritable bowel syndrome and associated complaints such as eczema.

A clinical study carried out at the Postgraduate Institute of Basic Medical Sciences, Madras, in 1990 tested the effectiveness of Gynema sylvestre, an Ayurvedic herb used in cases of hyperglycaemia. For the test 22 diabetic patients supplemented their conventional treatment with the herb extract for a period of 18 months, after which five were able to discontinue using their prescribed drugs. The remainder reported a noticeable improvement in their condition. It is thought that the herb regenerates the damaged cells, whereas conventional drugs simply slow the rate of damage.

Reading the aura

The aura is a multi-coloured field of etheric energy radiating around the body which is continually fluctuating to reflect changing emotions and state of health. It surrounds every living creature from single-cell organisms to humans, and extends even to inanimate objects which are composed of, and can absorb, energy.

Although invisible to the naked eye the aura can be seen by psychics, or sensitives as many now prefer to be called, and it can be recorded by high-frequency electronic photography known as Kirlian photography.

Anyone can develop the ability to see their own aura and the aura of others, but for practical purposes it can be useful to have a professional reading as an accurate diagnosis depends on more than simply knowing the meanings of the various colours.

Auric readings

Reading the aura is a natural heightening of awareness in which the reader simply looks beyond the physical form to the radiance of subtle energy surrounding the client. It involves a subtle shift of focus similar to that of altering your focus from an object which is near to you to one which is some distance away.

The first step in reading the aura is to hold a hand against a light neutral colour and to defocus slightly so that you are looking beyond the hand to the background. After a few tries you should be able to see a vivid blue outline about 2cm (¾in) around the hand.

This is the first layer known as the etheric aura and is a reflection of the life force. The strength of colour here is an indication of the general health of the individual.

The second layer is the emotional aura and extends about 10cm (4in) around the body. A predominantly active or intense personality, for example, will produce a red aura, while a clear green colour indicates emotional balance (see chakra balancing on page 157 for colour symbolism).

The third and fourth levels of the aura are more difficult for the inexperienced reader to see and even more difficult to distinguish between, as at this level there is a blending of the mental and spiritual energies. A spiritually evolved person will have a radiance of bright pastel colours around their head, an effect symbolized by the halo. Colour also emerges from key energy centres in the body which many aura readers are either unaware of or unable to see as their psychic sensitivity

Above: Each layer of the aura has its own colour, signifying health and emotional state.

and insight may not be developed enough.

An aura consultation

Usually the client will sit facing the reader and begin by talking about what concerns them at the moment. The client might also have a short list of questions that they would like to have answered and reading these aloud at the beginning could help the reader to tune in. After a few moments the average reader should be able to begin to describe the colours that they can see and what they reveal about the client's state of health in the past, the present and also in the immediate future. A more sensitive and knowledgeable reader will be able to make a more detailed interpretation that may even take in relevant details from past life experiences based on the indelible impressions left in the aura.

The primary benefit of an auric reading is the insights it

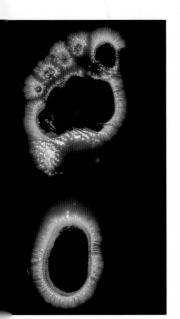

Left and far left: A technique known as Kirlian photography claims to be able to capture the aura on film.

can give into health and emotions. However, some highly sensitive psychics can see impressions of past events which can help to explain why the client's life has taken the direction that it has and what direction it is likely to take in the future.

Frequency of readings and safety

One session is usually enough to give a general picture of the client's emotional make-up, state of health and some basic guidance for their future health and happiness. But it may be useful to have further readings at times when significant decisions need to be taken, or if there is a persistent health or emotional problem.

Auric readings are perfectly safe from a physical point of view. The only danger arises if the consultant is unaware of, or unable to read, the subtler levels which help to give a wider, more accurate picture of the person as a whole and not just their physical health or emotions on the day of the reading. A genuine and responsible reader will also remind the client that the aura is a reflection of these various levels of the psyche and that their attitude and actions determine what is seen there. It should also be remembered that auric readings are not a means of foretelling the future.

Tai chi and chi kung

Tai chi is what is commonly known as a 'soft' martial art, a description which indicates that its aim is to develop inner strength and serenity rather than the channelling and application of physical force. Tai chi practitioners seek to achieve this state through a series of free-flowing movements which owe more to yoga and meditation than physical exercise. For this reason it is often referred to as 'meditation in motion'. Its ultimate aim is to promote longevity, a better quality of life and greater spiritual awareness. Regular practice of tai chi routines has proved very effective in increasing energy and stamina, releasing tension, relieving pain, healing minor injuries and improving physical flexibility and posture. On a more subtle level medical researchers have discovered that it can also help to stabilize the circulation, strengthen the immune system and stimulate the metabolism.

The origins of tai chi

The origins of tai chi are thought to date from between 960–1279 AD when a Taoist monk and martial arts expert, Chang San Feng, was inspired to integrate the actions of animals into his own martial arts routine (the 'hard' kung fu form tai chi chuan, which translates as 'the supreme way of the fist') after witnessing an encounter between a crane and a snake.

He combined the natural grace of the bird and the stealth of the snake with the characteristic actions of other animals in a series of graceful, stylized movements to create a repertoire of slow-motion routines. He also incorporated Taoist breathing techniques to stimulate the flow of chi, which subsequently evolved into the philosophy and practice of modern-day tai chi.

In more recent times the system has developed and divided into varied styles named after the masters who adapted them to their own rhythm and philosophy. The Yang form, for example, is slow, strong, rhythmic and flowing, while Chen is continually varied in pace and intensity.

How does it work?

The practical aspect of tai chi is the regular practice of 'the form'. There are long and short forms each of which comprises a set of slow-moving, stylized movements performed in a prescribed sequence. A typical long form involves 108 movements which takes between 20 minutes and one hour to complete. A short form varies between 24 and 48 movements, and rarely takes more than ten minutes to perform.

The movements are essentially self-defence sequences which mimic the movements of combat and take their names from imagined scenarios such as 'Repulse the Monkey' and 'Grasp the Sparrow's Tail'.

What happens in a class?

A typical class will begin with a minimum of ten minutes warming-up exercises before the instructor moves on to explaining and demonstrating the individual components of a particular form. It is not unusual for a class to spend up to a year learning a short form and possibly twice that to learn a long form, but once either has been mastered regular practice of that routine will ensure greater health and a sense of wellbeing for life.

A good instructor will explain the purpose behind the movements as well as demonstrating the technique, as it is as important to subscribe to the philosophy which the art seeks to express as it is to memorize all the movements.

Which problems can it help?

In addition to the benefits listed above tai chi can help to cure stress-related problems, reduce blood pressure, speed recuperation from surgery and serious illness and also alleviate the agony of arthritis and osteoporosis.

Chi kung

Chi kung or qigong, which translates as 'internal energy exercise', is a related system which teaches how to circulate energy with the minimum of movement. It focuses on cultivating an even disposition and maintaining general health rather than achieving a degree

of physical fitness. For that reason it could be considered a more gentle form of yoga. The exercises can be practised by people of any age and are suitable for those with physical disabilities, who are in ill-health or recuperating from illness and who are in need of a gradual return to activity.

The modern Master Lam Kam Chuen, author of The Way of Healing and Step-by-Step Tai Chi claims that ideally a chi kung exercise routine should be practised so slowly that anyone can stand still and become fit!

Above: The stylized movements of Tai Chi imitate the actions of animals and, in doing so, stimulate and direct the flow of chi to specific areas of the body.

Meditation

We all meditate, whether we are aware of doing so or not. Whenever our concentration wanders during a long journey, or when we find ourselves totally absorbed in a routine task to the exclusion of everything else, we are entering into an altered state of consciousness similar to that sought in meditation. On such occasions these experiences are little more than daydreams and the sense of detachment from physical reality is too fleeting to have a lasting effect. But accomplished practitioners believe that just ten minutes of regular, focused meditation every day leads to a significant improvement in health, emotional stability and a sense of wellbeing as well as numerous other benefits. Although it is thought to have originated in the East as a spiritual discipline, meditation has been universally practised in various forms by mystics and members of religious communities for thousands of years.

What is it?

Meditation is the quietening of the mind through either passive contemplation or heightened concentration. In its more advanced forms it is claimed to be an effective technique for altering one's state of consciousness from the ego or self-centred perspective to one which gives an increasing awareness of the real Self and of the oneness of all things.

Once the mind is stilled there is then the possibility of exploring the various levels of the psyche, delving into the uncharted regions of the unconscious and even raising the level of one's awareness to experience the inner and external dimensions of the spirit.

For therapeutic purposes it can be used to control the involuntary physiological functions such as the heart rate and body temperature, although these effects differ with the choice of technique being practised. This discovery led to the development of the biofeedback technique in the 1970s, a medical practic e in which patients copy meditation techniques for pain and stress relief.

How does it work?

Opinions differ as to whether the states of relaxation, heightened awareness and even ecstasy have a spiritual, mental, emotional or physical basis.

Scientific research carried out in the 1960s by Robert Wallace of the University of California and later by Harvard cardiologist Herbert Benson has shown that meditation has a more profound physiological effect than merely relaxing or even sleeping.

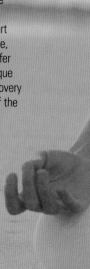

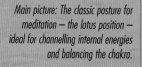

Main picture: The classic posture for meditation – the lotus position – ideal for channelling internal energies and balancing the chakra.

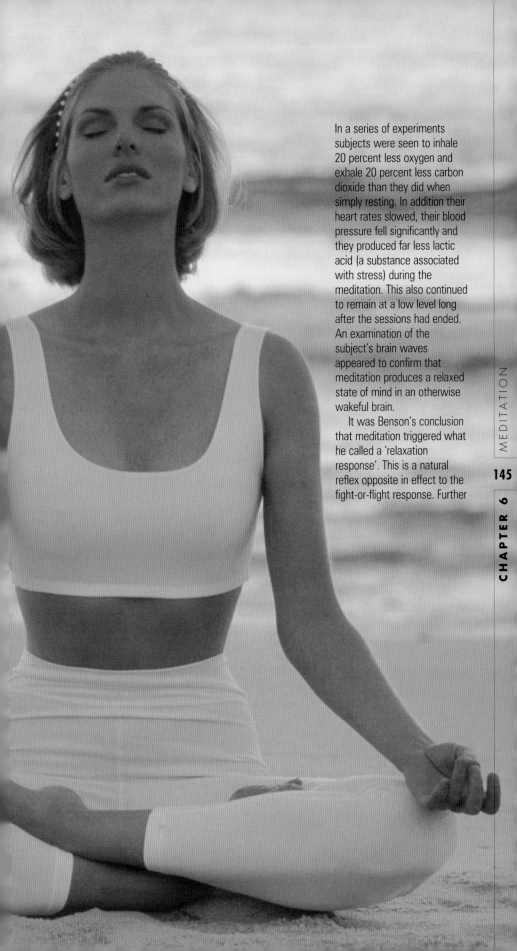

In a series of experiments subjects were seen to inhale 20 percent less oxygen and exhale 20 percent less carbon dioxide than they did when simply resting. In addition their heart rates slowed, their blood pressure fell significantly and they produced far less lactic acid (a substance associated with stress) during the meditation. This also continued to remain at a low level long after the sessions had ended. An examination of the subject's brain waves appeared to confirm that meditation produces a relaxed state of mind in an otherwise wakeful brain.

It was Benson's conclusion that meditation triggered what he called a 'relaxation response'. This is a natural reflex opposite in effect to the fight-or-flight response. Further

experiments in the 1960s by two Japanese researchers discovered that the brain waves of Zen monks dropped to the low theta frequency usually associated with sleep during their meditations while the monks remained acutely aware and awake.

What happens in a session?

If you are joining a group or class that does not follow a particular tradition you will be introduced to various techniques and encouraged to experiment with all of them until you find one that you feel comfortable with. Many Westerners feel too self-conscious to chant a mantra aloud, especially as these are invariably in Tibetan. If the teacher is sensitive to this they may instead suggest an affirmation in your own language, a positive saying which penetrates and influences the unconscious when it is repeated over and over again.

Another popular and effective method involves focusing your attention on a candle flame for a few minutes and then closing the eyes. The aim of this exercise is to keep the image of the flame in the mind's eye and in so doing still the thoughts which race through our minds using up mental energy to no effective purpose. Alternatively, those possessing a particularly vivid imagination may intuitively respond to a form of guided meditation known as active or creative visualization.These involve following a simple storyline narrated by the

discipline, develops intuition,
can assist the bereavement
process and, most important of
all perhaps, promises greater
peace of mind.

How many sessions are needed?

There is no set rule about the
number of meditation sessions
needed, but ten sessions
should be sufficient to show a
significant improvement in the
relief of stress and a greater
sense of wellbeing.

Is meditation safe?

Meditation is a perfectly safe
practice unless you have
recently experienced mental or
emotional problems or are
taking either prescribed or
illegal drugs. Those who are
nervous of encountering
psychic phenomena or are
worried about triggering
involuntary out-of-body-
experiences should first
concentrate on the grounding
exercises which are designed
to calm and balance the mind.
Meditation is not concerned
with such phenomena which,
incidentally, can occur at any
time. In such cases meditation
may prove beneficial in helping
to channel an over-active
imagination to a more positive
purpose.

If you have any doubts you
should first seek professional
medical advice.

teacher or group leader in the
mind, and afterward analysing
the images and symbols which
arise from the unconscious.
Not everyone feels comfortable
sharing their very personal
inner visions with a group and
you should never be put under
any obligation to do so.

Other techniques include
breath control and chakra
balancing. The latter involves
opening and harmonizing the
subtle energy centres in the
body to remove emotional or
energy blockages.

Which problems can it help?

On a purely physical level
research has proven that it can
reduce pain and be beneficial in
the treatment of anxiety,
migraine headaches and
cardiac arrhythmias.

Most of the methods
mentioned above are used
primarily for the relief of stress,
but they can be used as the
first steps in an inner journey
towards greater self-
awareness.

The regular practice of
meditation encourages self-

Transcendental Meditation

Above: Maharishi Mahesh Yogi, founder of TM and guru to the hippies of the 1960s.

This meditative technique was devised by Maharishi Mahesh Yogi (born 1911), a former physics graduate, factory worker and Hindu bhakti monk, who became famous when he briefly became guru to The Beatles in the late 1960s.

The Maharishi's initial idea was to develop a simple form of meditation for everyone, regardless of their religion. TM was to be neither a philosophy nor a religion, merely a 'natural, easy and scientifically verified technique'.

He taught that TM is founded on the 'eternal truth' at the core of all religions, that God is a universal force, not a cosmic father figure, that spiritual evolution involves each person living innumerable lives, and that human beings are essentially divine and can manifest their perfection through meditation.

What it involves

The TM-Sidhi programme, as it is officially called, promises to improve the practitioner's quality of life and to instil a lasting sense of inner peace. The technique involves using mantras which involve short words or phrases. The idea is to repeat these phrases in the mind to help calm normal thought processes and to reach a deep level of consciousness. The mantras are given to the TM practitioner according to their temperament and the life they lead. When chanted for 20 minutes at morning and evening devotions the mantras are believed to harmonize mind, body and spirit, resulting in a feeling of deep relaxation and a renewal of physical and mental energy.

Research into the psychological and physiological effects of meditation suggests that a deeper level of relaxation is achieved than during sleep. It is very good for alleviating stress as the technique seems to produce the opposite of the flight-or-fight response of the body. It helps to slow breathing, lowers blood pressure, reduces the heart rate and decreases the oxygen intake to bring serenity and stillness to the mind and body. People who regularly practise TM report having attained inner peace, and experiencing increased vitality and creativity.

Followers of Transcendental Meditation

For the two and a half million followers of Transcendental Meditation around the world traditional meditation is not sufficient to guarantee an adequate 'high'. They seek to obtain one of the sacred 'sidhis', or supernormal powers, of the Indian yogis: levitation. The stress placed on achieving this one ability above all others has earned the movement considerable criticism from Hindu yogis and ex-members of the movement, who claim to have experienced physical and mental problems as a result. And yet, the US military has undertaken a serious investigation of the movement's less flamboyant practices and expressed an interest in incorporating the techniques in its own training programmes.

If a significant number of members practise the technique together it is claimed that they will 'radiate an influence powerful enough to affect the whole of society'. A recent mass meditation in Washington led by TM members was said to have resulted in a 30 per cent fall in the crime rate throughout the city in the following months.

Critics of TM

However, critics condemn TM for promising the impossible — 'instant enlightenment'. They say that the 'true' path to enlightenment requires life-long and selfless devotion. While lengthy and regular meditation can be of great benefit as part of a balanced programme, if it is devoted exclusively to one self-centred ambition, such as levitation, it can become addictive and alienating, resulting, in extreme cases, in emotional and mental imbalance.

Feng shui

What is feng shui?

Feng shui (pronounced fung shoy) is the ancient Chinese art of living and working in harmony with the natural energies of the earth. The ancient Chinese believed that invisible energy, known as 'chi', flowed through us and everything around us, bringing all into balance. They also believed that everything contained yin (passive) and yang (positive) elements which needed to be adjusted to create harmony.

The flow of chi can unwittingly be blocked or diverted by environmental influences, poor planning or bad practice, and so disturb the harmony of our home or office. The aim of feng shui is to organize our personal environment so that this energy can flow freely and evenly, creating the best conditions for living a healthy and harmonious life.

Many multi-national companies such as Virgin, Body Shop, British Airways, BUPA, Citibank, and Chase Manhattan Bank have recognized the value of Feng Shui and incorporated it in their working environment. In many Asian cities it has become common practice for architects to consult feng shui experts to advise on the siting of a new building before construction even begins.

What can feng shui do for me?

Feng shui can be beneficial in almost every area of your personal and working life, although its principles can be used selectively for solving specific problems. It has been found to be particularly helpful for improving relationships, increasing concentration and creativity, attracting new opportunities and bringing financial security.

A fully qualified consultant will be able to identify those areas in your home or work place that appear to be influencing you adversely and will often suggest minor but effective changes that should help to restore balance and harmony, while also attracting the quality of energy that you need to fulfil your aspirations.

What happens in a consultation?

During a consultation, which can take anything from a couple of hours to a full day depending on the size of your property, you will be asked about the aspects of your life that you feel need improving. The consultant will then take an in-depth look at your living or working environment and recommend simple adjustments that you can make. They will identify areas where the energy appears to

be blocked or is flowing too quickly and suggest changes that will help the chi to flow freely and evenly.

Afterwards you often receive a more detailed written report and a plan for your home or office, showing the good and bad areas. It will take into account your personal needs, your temperament and can include the most appropriate colours for the different rooms, depending on the orientation.

Wherever possible, the cures used are simple and easy to implement.

Different techniques

Although most consultants base their advice on ancient theory alone, some claim to have a psychic sensitivity to atmosphere and can sensitize themselves to the energy blockages which they describe as being like musty cobwebs.

However, it is not only your personal space that will be analysed, but also your personality and potential. By studying the astrological influences some consultants will also advise which career you are most suited to, when the best time would be for moving house, committing yourself to a relationship and even which kind of people you should be looking to work with.

Some other aspects which can be taken into account during a consultation include: *Previous occupants* – by learning the past history of the property it is possible to discover its potential for influencing your life. For instance, if the previous occupants had personal, health or financial problems, then there is a possibility that you might experience similar difficulties, either because the uneven energy flow will continue to have a detrimental effect, or because the people themselves charged the atmosphere with their own negativity which will need to be dispelled. This principle applies to businesses too, and may account for the rapid closure of a series of shops using the same premises where negativity can have a cumulative effect.

In the event of the consultant detecting a pool of negativity, a technique called space clearing can be used to clear it and attract in new vital energy.

Kua numbers – by calculating your kua number (which is an expression of your personal energy pattern), the consultant can advise on the most auspicious directions for your bed, desk and other major fittings and furniture. By aligning yourself in harmony with these directions and avoiding the conflicting lines, you can increase good fortune in specific areas of your life.

Geopathic stress – your property will be checked for geopathic stress lines and underground streams. These lines of 'black energy' which can be measured and range in intensity from one to sixteen can have a detrimental effect on the health and psyche of those working or living directly above them.

Where geopathic stress is found, it can be cleared or deflected by using earth acupuncture. Normally a machine such as a raditec is recommended to do this, which creates an electromagnetic field to disperse the negative energy.

Below: The Bagua (or Pa Kua), an eight-sided figure depicting the eight compass points and the corresponding colours and elements used in feng shui.

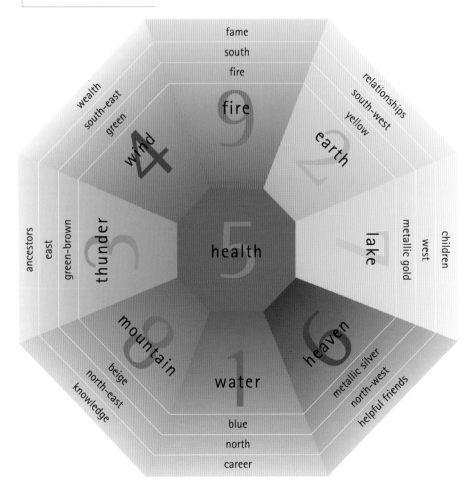

fame
south
fire

relationships
south-west
yellow

wealth
south-east
green

fire

earth

wind 4

9

ancestors
east
green-brown

thunder 3

health

5

lake 7

children
west
metallic gold

mountain 8

water 1

heaven 6

metallic silver
north-west
helpful friends

beige
north-east
knowledge

blue
north
career

Basic feng shui tips

If you do not have the time to study feng shui in depth, you can still get the chi energy working for you and improve your environment by following these five basic steps:

1 *Clear your clutter* Clutter obstructs the free flow of energy and can have a negative influence on your psyche. It is not only piles of dirty dishes and unwashed clothes that can have a depressing effect, but also items which you may have felt obliged to keep for some reason. Clutter is thought to accumulate from the fear of letting go of possessions and whatever they represent, so it is important to regard objects with detachment.

Clutter of any kind accumulates energy and leaves no space for new opportunities to enter your life. Unwanted objects can prove particularly depleting if you have charged them with your own emotions, such as those aroused by unhappy memories.

The rule to follow is: unless you love it or use it, it is clutter.

Having a good clear out is therapeutic, as is reorganizing the things that you value so that those you love are displayed to the best effect and those that you use can be easily located when you need them.

2 *Clean, tidy and in working order* While dust cannot be eliminated entirely, the accumulation of dirt and cobwebs suggest that the environment and the work done there is not sufficiently valued. Living or working in a dirty and dusty atmosphere can also have a subtle effect on your moods and attitude to work by expressing the unconscious belief that your efforts might be wasted, or that you might be overwhelmed by unreasonable demands.

Negative energy, frequently originating from your own frustrations, can become trapped in the mess and interfere with the flow of chi causing things to malfunction and ultimately break down entirely. Everything you rely upon should be kept in good repair as neglect can be costly both in purely financial terms and in terms of future good fortune, for example, leaking taps, broken machines or bulbs can foretell bad luck and loss of money.

If you have difficulties at

Main picture: The central principle of feng shui is the free-flow of energy and this is achieved with the minimum of clutter and conflicting lines.

work with a colleague or boss it can help to have a mirror on the desk to one side to reflect any negative energies towards a wall or window. This may sound like a simple superstition, but remember that a mirror has a metallic element which conducts the magnetic energy that radiates from all life forms.

3 *Toilets and bathrooms*

One of the key principles in feng shui is that energy seeks to return to the earth, just as lightning grounds itself by seeking out metal or trees. If you leave your bathroom or toilet door open and the toilet lid up, it is believed that energy will seep away through the water, which is also believed to relate to money.

4 *Plants*

The presence of a healthy plant with an upright growing habit will act as a focus for the chi energy and it will also help to circulate and purify both the energy and the air in the room. It is thought that some plants can also detoxify air which has been polluted by certain chemicals (including cigarette smoke, paint and the chemical agents used in aerosol sprays).

Flowering plants are particularly beneficial in a working environment as specific colours can stimulate the corresponding energy centres in the etheric body. For example, a deep blue bloom will have a calming effect, whereas a vivid red flower will stimulate the vital energy centres in the body, revitalizing those who are nearby.

Dried flowers are to be avoided as these are dead, and are incapable of contributing to the circulation process. Plants with spiky leaves are thought to disturb the flow of energy with their angular shapes, although some consultants believe spiky plants have yang energy.

Do bear in mind though that plants always require looking after and that dead plants are bad feng shui as they create negative energy.

5 *Entrances*

Many people leave their dustbins near the front door, which only serves to attract negative energy. Instead, try to keep them to the side, away from the house and place attractive flowers in pots or hanging baskets by the entrance. A clear, well-defined path or driveway that curves to follow the flow of chi, and a well-lit entrance attract opportunities, while a freshly painted front door in a bright, positive colour, will actively invite positive chi into your life.

Incidentally, doors should always open easily and nothing should be placed behind the door that would prevent it from being fully opened, obstructing this chi.

Whether you work from home or in an office, try to position your desk so that you do not have your back to the door. If this cannot be avoided then place a mirror or a reflective picture frame on the desk facing the door so that you can see people coming in.

By applying these simple, but effective remedies you should be able to improve the circulation and the quality of energy in your home and work place, helping you to work more efficiently, and bringing greater health and happiness.

Chakras

In the Eastern esoteric tradition, specifically yoga, our health, wellbeing and spiritual development are all dependent upon the functioning of our chakras. These are the invisible vortices of energy in the human body which are arranged along the spinal column connecting the etheric body to the physical. It is through the chakras that 'disease' of the mind and spirit is thought to manifest as physical symptoms in the body. However, by activating and balancing the chakras through various visualization techniques and the chanting of mantras we can improve our health, cleanse ourselves of negativity and even channel energy for the healing of others.

The seven major chakras

The root chakra (muladhara)
This is located at the base of the spine and is traditionally associated with the colours brown and black which correspond with the element of earth. One method of activating this chakra is to visualize it as a blossoming lotus flower whilst intoning the relevant mantram which is 'lam'.

The sacral chakra (svadhisthara)
This is located near the genitals and governs reproduction and physical action. It is traditionally associated with the colour red, the element of water and the mantram 'vam'.

The solar plexus chakra (manipura)
This is found above the diaphragm and is associated with the emotions. It is for this reason that the suppression of emotions usually results in stomach troubles. Stimulating and centring this chakra is said to improve the digestion and keep the liver, gall bladder and pancreas in good order. It is associated with the colour orange, the element of fire and the mantram 'ram'.

The heart chakra (anahata)
This is located in the centre of the chest. By stimulating this level of energy it is believed that we can awaken our capacity for expressing unconditional love which is one of the crucial stages in manifesting the divine spirit within. A fully functioning heart chakra regulates the blood flow and maintains the heart. The colour corresponding to the heart is green, the element is air and the mantram 'yam'.

The throat chakra (vishuddha)
This chakra governs communication, self-expression and creativity. The corresponding colour is blue, the element is the ether (in the form of sound vibrations) and the mantram is 'ham'.

The brow chakra (ajna)
This is found in the middle of the forehead between the brows which is believed to be the location of the third eye, the centre of psychic awareness. For this reason it is traditionally associated with the imagination, while on a physical level this chakra governs the pineal gland. Its corresponding colour is indigo, its element is light and its mantram is 'om'.

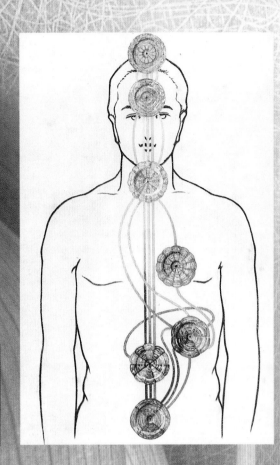

Right: The position of the chakras as they are traditionally envisaged in the Eastern esoteric tradition.

The crown chakra (sahasrara)

This is located above the head and governs the mental processes. It is associated with the colour violet and the element of thought, but it does not have a mantram. It opens when the other centres have been awakened in sequence.

In addition to the colours, elements and sounds that are traditionally associated with the chakras there are a number of other correspondences which reveal how the etheric body interconnects and affects our health and awareness.

For example, a gradual raising of consciousness from the physical to the spiritual levels finds expression in the verbs assigned to each chakra. 'I have' (root/the material world), 'I want' (sacral/desire), 'I feel' (solar plexus/emotions), 'I love' (heart/unconditional love), 'I speak' (throat/expression), 'I see' (brow/inner eye) and, I know' (crown/cosmic consciousness).

Stimulating the chakras

The chakras are continually responding to stimuli, although most of us are not conscious of it. For example, they slow down when we are depressed, which restricts the flow of energy and can cause illness, and they open wider when responding to specific stimuli relevant to each centre. A beautiful landscape, happy children or someone in distress might stimulate the heart centre, while an erotic image or the need for physical exertion will stimulate the sacral centre.

When we crave something at the expense of our higher nature we are effectively bringing ourselves down to the level of the sacral chakra and concentrating our energy at the basic primal animal level. Conversely, when we 'psych' ourselves up to do something requiring courage, we are unconsciously raising the energy level to the heart chakra, and when we steel ourselves for emotional difficulties we concentrate the energy at the solar plexus chakra. In meditation we open each of the chakras in turn from root to crown in order to centre them and open up to cosmic energy and the universal life force, which we can then draw down and channel into a specific chakra for healing.

Chakra balancing

Make yourself comfortable in an upright chair, with your feet flat on the floor parallel to your shoulders. Incline your chin slightly towards your chest and put your hands palm downwards on your thighs. Close your eyes and begin by focusing on your breathing.

When you feel sufficiently relaxed visualize yourself in a secluded walled garden with the brown earth beneath your feet. Feel the firmness of the solid ground supporting you, smell the delicate perfume of fresh flowers and cut grass and feel the warmth of the sun as it bathes your face and shoulders and then the rest of your body with light and revitalizing, healing energy.

Gradually become aware of the energy from the earth bringing a sensation of 'pins and needles' to the soles of your feet and travelling up through your ankles to the root chakra. From there it is absorbed into the sacral chakra beneath the navel where a red lotus flower emerges in response to the infusion of energy from the earth. Red is the colour of physical energy and visualizing a red lotus will help you draw upon vital energy to reinvigorate and revitalize every cell of your being.

Now visualize the energy from the red lotus rising upwards into the solar plexus chakra, the seat of the emotions, where it stimulates the opening of another flower. This lotus has a deep orange colour. Orange balances the red of physical energy with the yellow of the intellect. As this flower unfolds you may experience the release of suppressed emotions. Do not be surprised or self-conscious. Allow these feelings to be cleared and yourself to be cleansed of any negativity. Suppressing these emotions can only cause disease at one level or another.

Next imagine the light from the solar plexus chakra rising to merge with the light at the heart centre from where a fourth flower emerges. This lotus is green with a yellow centre. Yellow is symbolic of the sun, of healing and of the intellect, while green represents harmony and nature. This chakra is stimulated instinctively in response to natural beauty and brings compassion for all living things. Green is also symbolic of the border between the physical and spiritual realms,

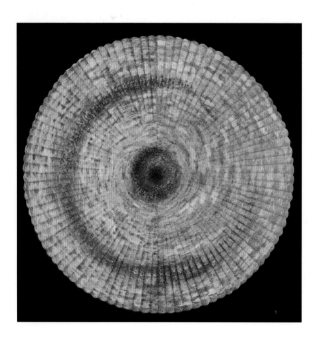

Left: The brow chakra illustrated by C.W. Leadbeater.

Above: A depiction of the crown chakra.

and so activating the chakras beyond this point helps raise awareness beyond the boundaries of the physical world.

Visualize the light from the heart centre rising to the throat chakra where a fifth lotus emerges. This flower has deep blue petals. Blue is the first of the spiritual colours and is symbolic of the level at which we are able to express our thoughts and feelings. As this lotus opens you may sense a tickling in the throat or a warm glow. With practice you may find that you are able to express yourself more clearly and with more confidence than before.

Now, visualize the light from the throat centre rising to the brow chakra in the middle of the forehead where a violet lotus is unfolding. Activating this centre can stimulate the psychic faculties and awaken communications from the unconscious. These inner visions usually appear in symbolic form, but don't be tempted to analyse them while you are meditating. Let them arise spontaneously and consider their significance later.

Finally, see the light from the brow rising to a point just above your head to activate the crown chakra. Visualize a pure white lotus emerging from the fountain of light which now rises up through the centre of your body and sense your awareness expanding.

Through the crown centre draw down cosmic energy into your body to merge with the light that is connecting and centring each of the seven chakras. Visualize yourself as a being of pure light with every cell of your being alive and invigorated. You have so much celestial and terrestrial power pulsing through your system that it begins to spill out of the crown and bubbles over, bathing you in a cascade of pranic (universal) energy that refreshes, invigorates and cleanses you from crown to toes. When the stream has subsided you are left in a deep state of relaxation and a more profound peace than you have ever known.

Gradually return to waking consciousness by counting slowly down from ten to one and becoming aware once again of the weight of your body sitting in the chair. When you are ready open your eyes and write down any impressions.

Reiki and Seichem

Healing is a natural extension of our instinctive urge to give comfort or relieve pain by placing our arm around someone's shoulder or putting a hand on the area that is sore, but some healers claim that they can be more efficient channels for the universal healing energy by training under specific disciplines.

Reiki and its complementary practice Seichem are ancient and unique forms of healing in that they require the healer to have experienced a course of attunements before they can act as a channel for the energy of the life force. It is from this force that Reiki takes its name: 'rei' meaning universal, and 'ki' meaning life energy. There are three levels that reiki practitioners can attain, first degree, second degree and third degree – master.

The origins of Reiki

The origins of Reiki are unknown, but it is said to have been rediscovered in the 19th century by Dr Mikao Usui, a Japanese scholar and Buddhist monk. However, it is now believed that Dr Usui's followers did not pass on to their trainees the full system during initiation which involved attuning to four healing rays corresponding to the elements of earth, air, fire and water. Modern Reiki only covers the healing energy connected to the earth element, whereas

Seichem uses all four.

The missing symbols and new initiation procedures are said to have been revealed to Kathleen Milner, a practising Reiki Master, through a series of consciousness-raising experiences. On testing these symbols and procedures, Milner found them to be stronger and more effective than the traditional ones that she had been using. Many other practitioners who have adopted the 'new' system confirm that Seichem offers more healing ability, increases the flow of energy and helps to 'open them up' psychically.

The healing energy

There is some controversy in the Reiki world over whether the 'new' symbols and methods are acceptable – the argument being that practitioners should stick with the system practised by Dr Usui. However, there is quite a lot of evidence to suggest that what was once regarded as traditional Reiki is not, in fact, the authentic Usui system.

A Reiki healer will also have undergone a 'clearing' process to make them a more receptive channel for the healing energy. This involves having their chakras balanced by a qualified and experienced Master of the technique who will also instruct them on all aspects of the therapy. These include the use of breath control to attune to

the patient, specific hand positions for directing the flow of energy into the body shown at the first degree level, and at the second degree level the use of certain symbols which are to be 'imprinted' in the patient's aura.

After their training and attunement it is claimed that healers need only express the intention to heal to connect with the universal life force. Whenever they give healing they will be directing the energy into the core of their patient's being where it will stimulate the innate ability of the body to heal itself and in doing so, restore the balance between mind, body and spirit.

The 21-day clearing process

With each attunement that Reiki students receive at the different levels their ability to channel energy increases, but to do so old patterns need realigning and blockages must first be cleared. These adjustments take a few weeks during which time the student may feel spaced out, have unsettling dreams, or may experience detoxification symptoms such as diarrhoea, sickness, a runny nose, or increased urination. Sometimes emotional issues may come to the surface which need to be resolved. If the process becomes uncomfortable then self-healing will help to rebalance the energy and decrease the symptoms.

Basic attunement

The first aspect of training involves a series of basic attunements during which the Reiki Master will use breathing techniques to build a reserve of

energy before 'drawing' certain
symbols above the crown of
the student's head. These are
then blown into the student's
aura and sealed. A similar
process will then be used to
place symbols into some of the
chakras. During this process
some students may see
colours, or images in their
mind's eye – while others
might experience an
overwhelming sense of peace
or be suffused with light. Some

may not be aware of anything
unusual during the attunement,
but should sense the Reiki
energy flowing through their
hands when they come to give
healing. From then on, the

ability to heal should stay for
life and intensify with practice.
As with other forms of healing
the energy can also be used on
pets and other animals and
even on plants. After achieving
the second degree level, it is
also possible to send 'absent
healing' to someone who is ill,
regardless of the distance,
through the medium of the
universal energy by just
thinking of the person or using
a photograph.

Reiki and Seichem workshops

A typical Reiki and Seichem workshop should cover the following:

Reiki 1 – *first degree training* At first degree training the following are usually discussed: the history of Reiki; how Reiki works; discussion of the 21-day clearing process; ethics; guided meditation; attunement; hand positions; group healing; self-healing; the nature of the chakras and chakra balancing; using Reiki to heal animals and plants; using Reiki to heal situations; practice of hands-on healing.

Reiki 2 – *second degree training* At second degree training the following are usually discussed: The three symbols – what they are and how they're used; the elements of Reiki meditation; attunement; distance healing with symbols; distant healing; other ways of using the symbols; combining Reiki with other therapies; charging crystals.

Seichem 1 – *first degree training* At first degree training the following are usually discussed: The history of Seichem; the Seichem rays: Sophi-el, Sakara and Angelic light; meditation and attunement; the chakras and how to work with them; magnetic healing; opening and closing the aura; etheric surgery; working with guides.

Seichem 2 – *second degree training* At second degree training the following are usually discussed: The Seichem symbols – what they are and how to use them; additional symbols; meditation and attunement; practice using the symbols to heal people and situations; cutting emotional ties; using the violet flame.

The third degree level is to become a Reiki or Seichem Master so that you can attune new initiates. Few people reach this level as the course is very expensive and the person needs to have a mature outlook on life and a deep spiritual awareness.

The benefits of Reiki and Seichem

Reiki and Seichem were developed for healing both the practitioner and the patient, for giving full body treatments, and for treating specific ailments, although it can be used simply

Main picture and right: Reiki and Seichem specify particular positions for hands-on-healing, rather than the intuitive impromptu methods of traditional 'faith healing'.

as a periodic 'top up' to increase the sense of wellbeing and to maintain good health. Once you have had Reiki and Seichem attunement and are familiar with the techniques you can give yourself a treatment wherever you are, even in a supermarket queue or on a bus, to set yourself up for the day.

It is an entirely safe system for treating many acute ailments and chronic conditions including pre-menstrual tension, back pain, eczema, arthritis, sinusitis, cystitis, migraine headaches, asthma, menopausal problems, ME (chronic fatigue syndrome) and sciatica.

But it is not only physical ailments which can be helped. Healing is holistic by nature and can be directed to anything which is disturbing the balance of energy in the body or psyche. Emotional problems, difficulties with relationships, fears, phobias, depression, insomnia, minor addictions such as overeating and smoking, general anxiety and stress can all be helped.

The healing can be directed into the past to alleviate regrets or to dispel negative conditioning which is preventing the practitioner or patient from attracting new opportunities, and also into the future (for example, to the venue where you will be taking an exam or will be interviewed for a job).

What happens during a treatment session

Before the first treatment session the patient will be asked basic medical details and their reasons for coming for healing. They will also be introduced to the basic principles of Reiki so that they know what to expect and how it might benefit them. This discussion will add about half an hour to the standard treatment time of one hour.

During treatment the healer will ask the recipient to lie on the treatment table while they place their hands for 3–5 minutes on the key energy centres from the head down to the base of the spine, on both sides of the body in an unbroken, flowing movement.

It is not of course necessary to practise Reiki or Seichem in order to heal, but it can be more focused and very effective, particularly with the use of the Reiki symbols. When used in combination with other therapies Reiki has been found to increase their potency.

But perhaps the greatest benefit is also the most subtle – the increased awareness which comes with being attuned to the universal spirit.

Acupuncture

Acupuncture, which translates as 'needle piercing', is the ancient Chinese practice of inserting very fine needles into the skin at key pressure points to increase the flow of vital energy (chi) around the body. Its uses range from preventing and treating disease, to relieving pain and even anaesthetizing patients for surgery.

The earliest written account of acupuncture appears in the Nei Jing – The Yellow Emperor's Classic Of Internal Medicine, which is thought to date from 200 BC, making it the oldest surviving medical text book. However, the practice could be even older still, possibly originating as early as 3,000 years before the establishment of Christianity.

How does it work?
There are a number of theories which seek to explain the evident effectiveness of acupuncture, but it is believed that the needles stimulate the nervous system releasing endorphins, the body's natural painkillers. On a more subtle level the needles are thought to dissolve energy blockages in the etheric body which prevent sufficient chi from reaching the vital organs causing disharmony and disease. In this way acupuncture effectively helps to restore the pattern of inner harmony.

The concept of chi
Chi is believed to flow throughout the body through invisible channels known as meridians. There are 12 main meridians and innumerable minor ones, just as there are blood vessels serving a network of tiny capillaries in the physical body. Of the 12 major meridians six are designated as yin (dark, negative and passive) and six are yang (light, positive and active), each set needs to be in balance with each other. The 365 main acupuncture points are ranged along the meridians. Each is traditionally identified by a name and a number. For example, 'Leg Three Miles' is the name for stomach point 36 (St 36) and 'Bright and Clear' is gall bladder point 37 (GB 37).

The free flow of chi ensures that the body is balanced and healthy, but if the energy becomes blocked, it is thought that the vital organs are starved of energy and either the body will develop symptoms of disease or the person will develop signs of mental or emotional ill-health such as depression, anger, self-pity or irrational fear. The Chinese identify other factors which can contribute to the ill-health of a person, which they call 'the six pernicious influences'. These are wind, dryness, cold, fire, humidity and summer heat.

The Chinese holistic view of health also encourages us to take responsibility for our own health and wellbeing by keeping to a healthy diet, reducing stress from overwork and taking regular exercise.

What happens in a consultation?
The Chinese treat illness holistically as an expression of disharmony of the mind, body and spirit. To arrive at a diagnosis, the acupuncturist

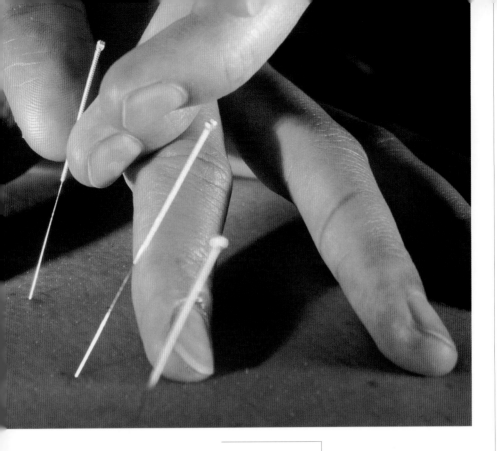

seeks to identify a weak link in the energy chain.

The initial consultation will be taken up with a detailed diagnosis. The acupuncturist will ask questions about your personality, your lifestyle, your work, general health and that of your family. You may even be asked about your pastimes, if they suspect that these might be relevant.

Your appearance, posture and facial colour are also significant indicators of your inner state. An examination of your eyes will signify the condition of shen (or spirit). Bright, shiny eyes indicate that shen is in harmony with the body, whereas lustreless eyes

Left: Acupuncture needles act like conductors to release energy blockages and improve circulation.

Above: Acupuncture needles are quite painless and are left in position for up to 20 minutes.

are a sign of disharmony. The colour and condition of the tongue, breath and tone of your voice will also be examined.

Treatment is given with the patient lying on a couch and undressed sufficiently to allow access to the relevant points of the body. Between four and eight needles are usually considered sufficient for most ailments. These are inserted to different depths and left in for anything between a few seconds and half an hour. Usually the patient feels no more than a tingling or numbness on insertion. Although it is possible to feel an immediate improvement after treatment, it is more common to feel the benefits after a few days.

How many sessions do I need?

The length of treatment varies according to the type and severity of the illness, the patient's age, and their response to treatment, but there should be a noticeable improvement after three sessions.

Which problems can it help?

Acupuncture has been proven to be beneficial in treating acute (short-term) conditions, most types of aches and pains, from arthritis to back pain, and even pre-menstrual tension. It has also been effective in reducing stress, alleviating depression and stimulating the circulation. It can also help gynaecological problems, bronchial ailments such as hay fever and asthma and unspecified complaints such as ME and fatigue.

Chinese herbal medicine

In Chinese medical philosophy acupuncture and herbalism are seen as the expressions of the complementary principles yin and yang and are both part of the ancient system of traditional Chinese medicine (TCM). Acupuncture is considered the equivalent of yang, because it influences chi from the outside, while herbalism is seen as yin, because it redresses the balance of mind, body and spirit from within by adding nourishment to the body which in turn rebalances the psyche and the spirit.

Chinese herbal medicine is often used to complement acupuncture, to speed recovery, although it can be used by itself for disorders such as anaemia, viral infections, menstrual problems and skin diseases such as eczema.

But while the Chinese use a combination of whole herbs or a concoction of several herbs Western pharmaceutical companies invariably extract the active ingredients from the herbs and use them to suppress the symptoms of disease. So, to test the effectiveness of the treatment it is recommended that a patient consults a qualified professional Chinese herbalist for a comprehensive diagnosis rather than relying on a manufactured concoctions that are available over the counter. It is also possible that the ailment is a symptom of a fundamental imbalance which only a qualified and experienced practitioner would be able to identify.

How does it work?

The herbs restore the natural balance of elements and energy within the body which may have been adversely affected by internal and external influences such as emotional problems, stress, poor diet and environmental factors. The environmental factors are what the Chinese term 'the six pernicious influences': wind, dryness, cold, fire, humidity and summer heat.

The herbs have specific properties such as warming, dissipating damp, neutralizing wind and regulating blood pressure and so can restore warmth to cold chi, for example, or move stagnant chi by exerting a specific effect on the meridian responsible for the imbalance.

What happens in a consultation?

The consultation and diagnosis is similar to that given by a TCM acupuncturist. The practitioner will pay particular attention to your anatomical type, general manner and posture, the tone of your voice, your breath, pulse, the colour of your face, the condition of your tongue and the eyes.

Facial colour can be significant: a white face indicates an imbalance in the metal element, a yellowish complexion is related to the earth element, while a ruddy complexion is a sign of an imbalance in the fire element.

The colour and condition of the tongue is another significant indicator of health and inner harmony. A red tongue with a moist, thin whitish coating called 'moss' is a healthy sign while a purplish tinge suggests that chi is stagnant. A deficiency of chi shows up as a thick coating of 'moss' and an excess as a thin coating. The different regions of the tongue correspond to the vital organs and can therefore indicate problems in these areas: the tip corresponds to the heart, the middle of the tongue to the spleen, the root to the kidneys and the sides to the liver and gall bladder.

How many sessions do I need?

Minor ailments can clear up within a week and so one consultation might be enough, but for more serious conditions half a dozen treatments over six months are usually necessary. This allows the herbs time to work through the system and initiate the regeneration of cells so that they bring about a significant improvement.

Left: Chinese herbs are natural plant extracts but should only be taken under medical supervision.

Which problems can it help?

The World Health Organization has published a list of ailments which can benefit from Chinese herbalism. These include arthritis, depression, eczema, hay fever, infertility, sciatica, herpes, insomnia, PMS, vaginitis, cerebral palsy, diabetes and even strokes.

Addictions can also be cured in certain cases. American scientists have discovered that the root of the Chinese herb kudzu vine, for example, which is a traditional Chinese treatment for alcoholism, contains chemicals that suppress the desire for alcohol.

Is it safe?

Chinese herbs are now widely available to buy over the counter, but although many are harmless it is strongly recommended that anyone with more than a minor ailment should submit to a full examination by a qualified practitioner. Although the herbs are natural plant extracts and free of side-effects, some herbs are safe to use only in specified doses.

Main picture: The Chinese use a combination of whole herbs or a mixture of herbs to treat the patient holistically.

Naturopathy

Naturopathy is an ancient, multi-disciplinary holistic system of healthcare the central philosophy of which is that 'nature heals'. It rejects all synthetic drugs in favour of a natural lifestyle which incorporates periodic fasting, hydrotherapy, routine exercise, an organic diet, regular relaxation and selective manipulative techniques. Naturopathy was regarded as a fringe therapy until the early 20th century, when prominent naturopaths such as Dr Henry Lindlahr, Stanley Lief and Alfred Vogel became concerned at the amount of drugs that were being freely prescribed by orthodox practitioners. In contrast, the naturopaths promoted the idea that the secret of achieving and sustaining good health was to live a healthy lifestyle and to treat any ailments with natural compounds in the belief that nature has all the cures that we need.

The three principles of naturopathy
Naturopathy is founded on three basic principles:
The existence of a vital force: Naturopaths believe that the body contains a 'vital curative force' which, if kept in a healthy condition, will fight disease and aid recuperation, enabling the body to return to a state of equilibrium known as homoeostasis. In this sense naturopathy is not a system of combating infection, but of preserving a state of physical, mental and emotional wellbeing.

Naturopaths accept disease as a natural phenomenon: Many illnesses and infections are not only seen as being inevitable but also as a valuable aid in helping to build a strong immune system. Viral infections such as flu, and childhood illnesses such as chickenpox are considered a necessary stage in an individual's development from infancy to maturity, and so naturopaths are against vaccination in principle. Experience has shown that colds and flu which are allowed to work their way through the system can reduce the risk of bronchitis or degenerative diseases such as arthritis in later life. But while mild diarrhoea, for example, is seen as the body's method of ridding itself of toxins, it is important to identify which illnesses can be prevented and act accordingly to eliminate the risk of re-infection. Illnesses which can be avoided are usually those which are the result of poor diet, inefficient elimination of body wastes, physical injury, hereditary factors, negative emotions, lack of exercise and environmental pollutants.

The symptoms of disease: These are seen as signs that the healing process is taking place and that the vital force is striving to balance the body. For that reason naturopath practitioners do not prescribe compounds to suppress symptoms in healthy individuals. The responsibility of the naturopath is to aid the body in its fight by strengthening the immune system rather than interfering in the natural healing process.

The triad of health
Good health depends on maintaining a balance between the body's anatomy, its biochemistry and the emotions. The health of the nervous system and internal organs can be adversely affected by poor posture, brittle bones, flabby muscles, strained tendons and

torn ligaments. Biochemical health refers to nutrition which is essential for growth, cell regeneration and immunity to disease. Poor nutrition can be physically damaging because it can upset the chemical balance in the body and pollute the cells with toxins. Strong emotions such as fear, hate or resentment can also adversely affect health by disrupting the digestion, causing hormone imbalance and upsetting the body's biochemical balance.

Which problems does it help?

Naturopathy can help with many acute (short-term) and chronic (long-term) problems, such as anaemia, allergies, arthritis, bronchitis, candida, circulation disorders, constipation, cystitis, eczema and other skin diseases, irritable bowel syndrome, migraine, PMS, sinusitis and ulcers. It can also improve the body's resistance to infections.

What happens in a consultation?

A naturopathy diagnosis is similar to one by an orthodox doctor in that it involves taking the pulse and blood pressure,

Above: A natural balanced diet supports the body's vital curative force.

listening to heart and lungs and assessing lung capacity. In addition, naturopaths will determine which of the three standard physical types you belong to as each is prone to different ailments and will require a special diet to prevent these occurring.

This diagnosis according to type is known as biotypology. The endomorph type is soft and round; the mesomorph is more muscular and of stocky build, while the ectomorph has a long and lean shape. Endomorphs, for example, can be prone to gall bladder problems, mesomorphs can suffer degenerative arthritis, while ectomorphs are susceptible to rheumatoid arthritis.

Other elements of the diagnosis can include an iridology check – where the condition of the iris of each eye will be examined for other body problems, mineral analysis –

samples are taken from hair and sweat and bioelectronic analysis – this process tests energy levels electronically.

Treatment

Diet: A typical treatment will include a short fast to eliminate any toxins, a gentle exercise routine, followed by a change of diet. The latter will be designed to eliminate processed foods and replace them with vegetarian and organic wholefoods with plenty of raw fruit and vegetables whose nutritional content has not been destroyed by cooking.

Hydrotherapy: Alternate hot and cold baths or showers can be prescribed to stimulate the circulation, relieve pain and help to remove congestion. In addition, extra treatment might involve osteopathy to restore flexibility to joints and muscles and improve posture and, in certain cases, a course of psychotherapy may also be recommended to reduce any psychological pressures.

Reflexology

Reflexology is commonly associated with acupuncture, but in practice the two forms of therapy have little in common. Both are believed to have originated in China and both seek to influence the flow of energy, but acupuncture uses needles at numerous points on the body to stimulate energy flow, while reflexology concentrates exclusively on manipulating pressure points on the soles of the feet to remove any blockages.

One theory suggests that every vital organ, gland and muscle group corresponds to a specific region on the sole of the foot. When illness occurs anywhere in the body it is said that crystalline deposits form beneath the skin on the sole of the foot in the corresponding zone. By massaging the foot the reflexologist aims to break down the crystals and restore the circulation of electro-chemical energy to the affected area. Another theory attributes its evident effectiveness to the possibility that the massage triggers a reflex action in a related muscle or organ. Medical science has identified over 70,000 nerve endings on the sole of each foot which are linked to all areas of the body and brain via the autonomic nervous system. By applying pressure to these nerve endings it is possible to increase the flow of nutrients and oxygen around the body and eliminate toxins much more efficiently. But this is a physical reflex. It is not certain that there is a corresponding network in the 'subtle', or etheric body which could account for the more dramatic effects on health and wellbeing.

Westerners who are brought up to believe that treatment should be given at the point of pain tend to be sceptical about the effectiveness of a consultation, but the results are impressive. It has been shown that pregnant women who recently underwent a course of reflexology in Britain were in labour for half the average period. There have been similar claims from studies made of people suffering from muscle strain, headaches, sciatica, gastrointestinal problems and premenstrual syndrome (PMS). It is also believed to help reduce the side-effects of chemotherapy, relieve the severity of asthma attacks, alleviate depression and reduce inflammation and eliminate stress.

The feet as a reflection of the body

Reflexologists subscribe to the belief that the body is mirrored in the features of the feet. If you lie down with your feet together the toes will correspond to the head and neck; the balls of the feet to the upper torso and internal organs; the area from the ball of the feet to the middle of the arch to the region from the diaphragm to the waist; the middle of the arch to the heel will correspond to the waist and pelvic region; and the heels to the pelvic area and the sciatic nerve. The curves of the spine are mirrored in the inner curve of each foot, the outer contour to the arms, shoulders, hips, legs, knees and lower back as the line descends, while the ankle corresponds to the pelvic region and the generative organs.

DIY treatment

Before treating yourself it may be wise to go for a professional consultation to become familiar with the positions of the main pressure points. But you can treat yourself for many simple ailments using the steps outlined below.

Rest your bare right foot on your left leg and 'work' the entire surface of the skin before concentrating on a specific area that you feel needs special attention.

Reflexologists work the soles of the feet using the edge of the thumb and the fingertips, either by 'walking' the thumb or finger across the reflex point using a caterpillar-like movement during which the hand does not lose contact with the foot, by rotating the thumb into the relevant point while supporting the foot with the other hand, or by flexing the foot with the free hand while pressing the point with the thumb.

To treat headaches:
Thumb- or finger-walk all over the pad of the big toe. If a

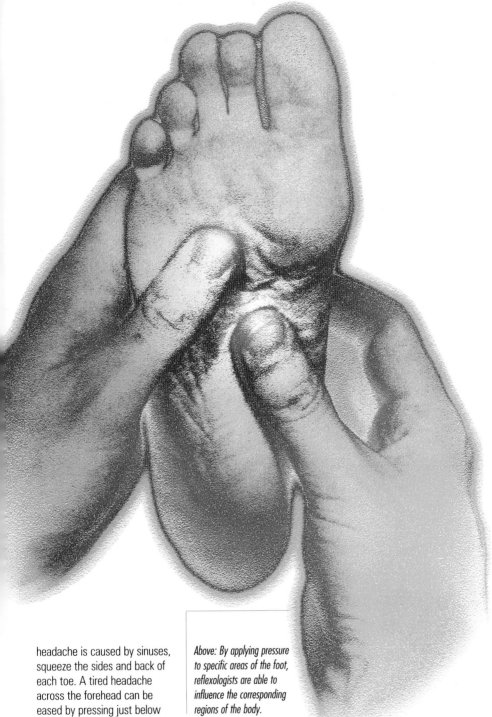

headache is caused by sinuses, squeeze the sides and back of each toe. A tired headache across the forehead can be eased by pressing just below the big toenail.

To treat period pains: Heavy and painful periods are best treated with an entire reflexology session. Special attention could be paid to the ovaries, pituitary and spine whose points are found between the ankle bone and the back of the heel on the outside of the foot, the centre

Above: By applying pressure to specific areas of the foot, reflexologists are able to influence the corresponding regions of the body.

of the pad under the big toe and the outside of the side of the foot.

To treat stress: Rotate the thumb into the solar plexus area; in the centre of the underneath of the foot.

Herbalism

Herbalism is one of the oldest forms of medical treatment and is the most widely practised. It is fundamental to the healthcare and culture of Africa, Asia and remote parts of Europe and South America where the curative properties of plants, flowers, trees and herbs are used to restore and maintain the body's natural balance rather than simply suppress the symptoms. Herbalism is currently enjoying a revival in the West where it is seen as a viable alternative to the use of drugs, which can produce side-effects, kill healthy bacteria and so exacerbate infections.

For example, a herbalist will prescribe garlic for certain digestive disorders because it is a natural antibiotic. It invigorates the flora (micro-organisms) in the gut which then acts more efficiently and thereby the risk of re-infection is reduced. Conventional antibiotics may eliminate the infection but they also disturb the balance of the flora.

The healing properties of certain herbs have been accepted as a fact by orthodox medicine for more than a century – steroids, amphetamines, aspirin and digitoxin all originate from herbs – as did most of the drugs used in the first half of the 20th century. But in trying to reproduce or synthesize the dominant active ingredient, pharmaceutical companies have tended to ignore the secondary ingredients which aid recovery. In contrast, the herbalist understands that a herbal concoction is greater than the sum of its constituent elements, an approach known as synergism.

How do they work?

Herbs are composed of mutually dependent chemicals which are most effective when the active elements are used whole and in their natural state. These include vitamins, minerals, carbohydrates, trace elements and healing agents such as bitters, tannins, glycosides, volatile oils, saponins, alkaloids and mucilage. These fight infection, relax tense muscles, sedate overactive organs and nerves, stimulate circulation and reduce inflammation.

When the body's own 'vital force' is weakened by stress, poor nutrition and other factors the whole system is thrown out of balance. What we perceive as symptoms of a specific illness, the herbalist will view as signs of the healing process and prescribe whatever they feel is appropriate to support the immune system, speed the detoxification process, and prevent a recurrence of the disease. Though they will consider what is the most appropriate treatment for the patient rather than the illness.

Herbal remedies are available as tablets, capsules, tinctures, creams, compresses, poultices, infusions, decoctions and even bath oils. It is also possible to take them as fresh herbs to add to your food. It is important to understand that the remedy might make you feel worse before you notice an improvement. This is common to many natural therapies and results from the detoxification and rebalancing process that occurs.

What happens in a consultation?

The initial consultation can take up to an hour as the herbalist will require a comprehensive medical history and a personality profile. It could be that the current ailment relates to a previous problem so the overall picture is important for an accurate diagnosis. The initial consultation will take account of posture, skin tone

Left: Herbalism was once associated with witchcraft but is now enjoying a revival as a complementary therapy.

and the condition of your hair and may also include a traditional check-up to test reflexes, heart beat and blood pressure. In addition to the herbal prescription that you will receive, you may also be advised on diet, exercise and relaxation routines.

How many sessions will I need?

A minor ailment can be cleared up in a few days which means that only one appointment might be necessary, but chronic conditions can require a course of treatment and consultations over several months.

Above: Herbal remedies are generally safer than pharmaceutical drugs and have no side effects.

Which problems can it help?

Herbalism has proven to be particularly effective in treating inflammatory skin conditions such as eczema, digestive problems such as irritable bowel syndrome and urinary conditions such as cystitis.

Fractures and other physical problems requiring surgery are not suitable for this form of treatment, however, herbalism can alleviate the discomfort and emotional stress generated by these more severe ailments.

Are they safe?

Herbal remedies have been proven to be generally safer than pharmaceutical drugs, but they must be taken under medical supervision and only in the dose prescribed. They should only be taken by the person for whom they were prescribed for the reasons already stated. Some remedies are available over the counter and are perfectly safe for children and pregnant women, but there are some herbs which are toxic when taken in large doses and whose sale is regulated by law.

Aromatherapy

Aromatherapy was widely used in the ancient world. The Romans, Egyptians and Greeks used aromatic oils mainly for bathing and massage, but also to ward off disease. Hippocrates, the Greek father of medicine, rid Athens of the plague by the judicious use of aromatic fumigations. However, the term aromatherapy (meaning 'treatment with scent') did not come into common usage until the 1930s when a French chemist, René-Maurice Gattefosse, accidentally discovered the therapeutic use of essential oils after burning his hand during an experiment. In desperation he plunged it into a container of lavender oil which to his surprise sped up the healing process and the injury left no scar.

A growing therapy

Since then aromatherapy has become the fastest growing complementary therapy in Britain, where it is used extensively in clinics, hospitals, hospices, beauty salons and therapy rooms as well as in private homes. It has proven a safe and effective form of pain relief for women in labour and for patients suffering the side effects of chemotherapy. Industry too has begun to

discover the potential benefits. In Japan it is becoming common practice to install aroma systems into new commercial premises where customers will be calmed by essence of rosemary and lavender and staff will be stimulated to stay alert with the fragrances of eucalyptus and lemon.

Approximately 150 essential oils have been extracted from flowers, plants, trees, fruit, bark, grasses and seeds and identified as having a unique healing property which can improve health, alleviate psychological and physiological problems and prevent illness. All of these oils have been found to have specific properties which mean that they can be prescribed according to the patient's needs. Some are anti-viral, anti-inflammatory, anti-depressant, pain-relieving, antiseptic, stimulating, relaxing, and of diuretic value. They have

Above: The essences of certain flowers have been found to have a calming effect.

all of the healing properties but none of the side effects of pharmaceutical drugs. The only disadvantage to aromatherapy appears to be cost, as some of the rarer essences can be very expensive to produce in quantity and synthetic copies are known to be ineffective.

How do they work?

Research indicates that there are at least 100 different chemical compounds in each essential oil which have a specific effect on the mind and body. For example, aldehydes calm the nerves, phenols aid regeneration and alcohols are stimulants. Others have several uses depending on what the body requires at that time and for that reason these are known as adaptogenics.

lemon, lavender or cypress oil diluted in a footbath.

Compresses: A piece of cotton soaked in a solution of lavender oil and water and laid on a bruise, sprained muscle or skin disorder for a couple of hours can bring significant relief from discomfort.

Applying oil on the skin: Although a number of oils are not suitable to apply directly to the skin, there are some, such as lavender, which can significantly reduce the pain and shock of a burn when applied undiluted. Tea tree is also very effective on insect bites and minor cuts.

Taken internally: Essential oils are sometimes prescribed to be taken internally, but this is rare and only done under strict medical supervision. As a general rule oils are not recommended for consumption as they can have serious adverse effects on health.

Which problems can it help?
Aromatherapy has been found to be particularly effective against stress, headaches, depression, irritability, digestive disorders, muscular pains, rheumatism and gynaecological problems, although it is not recommended during pregnancy, or for those who suffer from allergies, high blood pressure or epilepsy.

How are the oils used?
There are seven methods of treatment; inhalations, diffusers and vaporizers, massage, baths, compresses, applying oil on the skin and internally.

Inhalations: This method can be as simple as sleeping on a pillow or breathing from a handkerchief that has absorbed a few drops of the required essence, or inhaling deeply from a steaming solution in order to clear congestion.

Diffusers and vaporizers: These distribute the fragrance into the air so that one can effectively breath in the benefit while doing some other task, although it is advisable to use an electrical diffuser in a bedroom rather than a candle burner or ceramic ring because of the risk of fire.

Massage: This is the form favoured by the majority of aromatherapists as the benefit of the oil (which is normally diluted in sweet almond or grapeseed oil) is increased by the therapeutic effect of touch, releasing trapped energy, stimulating circulation and relieving tension and stress.

Baths: These can be scented with essential oils or a shower can be rounded off with an invigorating rubdown with a flannel impregnated with half a dozen drops of grapefruit oil. Chilblains and tired feet can be helped by a few drops of

Main picture: Aromatherapy has proven to be a safe and effective form of pain relief.

Homoeopathy

Although the principles of homoeopathy were known to the 5th-century Greek physician Hippocrates they were not developed into the alternative, holistic form of medicine that we are familiar with today until the 18th century. The German physician and chemist Samuel Hahnemann made the discovery that was to turn the rules of orthodox medicine on their head after doing some experiments with quinine. Dr Hahnemann knew that quinine was effective against malaria, but he doubted the orthodox view which credited the drug's success to its astringent properties. Over the course of several days he took quinine and recorded his reactions which included malaria-like symptoms, despite the fact that he was not infected with the disease. When he stopped taking the drug the symptoms ceased and when he resumed the dosage they returned. He concluded that quinine was effective against malaria because it could simulate those symptoms and cause the body's natural immune system to react against them. As with other drugs, quinine acted as a trigger, not a cure. It was the immune system which effected the cure. So Hahnemann reasoned that it must also be possible to cure a multitude of psychobiological problems by 'fooling' the body into thinking that it was under threat so that it would redress its natural balance without the patient resorting to conventional drugs.

How does it work?

Homoeopathy is the antithesis of conventional medicine in that it helps the body to heal itself by treating 'like with like', rather than giving an antidote. Hahnemann believed that nature does not permit two diseases of a similar type to exist in the body simultaneously so homoeopathy introduces an artificial disease similar to that from which the patient is suffering in the belief that the body will cancel out the real one. In practice, a patient who is in perfect health at the time of the consultation is given a substance that will manifest the symptoms of a particular illness or psychological disorder from which they suffer periodically.

For example, a doctor will prescribe a drug that causes constipation to a patient suffering from diarrhoea, while a homoeopathic practitioner will prescribe a substance with a minute trace of a substance that would normally cause diarrhoea if given in a larger dose.

There are over 2,000 homoeopathic remedies many of them sourced from animals, vegetables and minerals, all of which are diluted to such a degree that even the most toxic substances carry no risk of side-effects. The technique of dilution is known as 'potentizing' and involves dissolving the natural ingredients in a solution of alcohol and water which is left to stand for between two to four weeks. During this time the solution is periodically shaken and strained to leave what is known as the mother tincture. This is then diluted and shaken, or 'succussed' a number of times until not a single molecule of the original ingredient remains, only its 'vibrational pattern' remains imprinted in the solution. The remedies are supplied in different dilutions as granules, pills, powder or lactose tablets.

According to what are known as the Laws of Cure the body heals itself in reverse order, so that the last symptoms to appear will be the first to disappear. It is common for patients to feel emotionally better before feeling physically better, although it is also common for the patient to feel slightly worse before feeling better as the illness works its way out of

Above: Samuel Hahnemann discovered the effectiveness of potential cures after subjecting himself to a series of illnesses.

history. Usually one or two further half-hour visits are necessary to check on progress and perhaps to prescribe another remedy if the first choice is not effective or another remedy is required for a related disorder.

When the remedy has been prescribed, the homoeopath will advise on how it should be taken as this is an important element of the treatment. You will be told not to touch the pills but to place them under the tongue and allow them to dissolve. Coffee, peppermints and conventional toothpaste are to be avoided during the treatment as these can alter its effectiveness. A mild fennel toothpaste is often recommended as a replacement during the course of treatment.

What problems can it help?

Homoeopathy does not work for everybody, but it is effective for most types of illnesses and psychological problems. Minor ailments such as colds, diarrhoea and constipation can clear up very quickly, while patients suffering from more chronic conditions such as rheumatoid arthritis, psoriasis, asthma, migraine and fibrositis can respond gradually to treatment over a longer period.

the system. The last law states that healing takes place from the head downwards, working from the major to the vital organs before improved health is shown from the inside out.

What happens in a consultation?

A homoeopath makes a diagnosis based on the person and how they respond to the disease, not the disease itself. In the initial consultation, which can last up to an hour, they will compile a 'whole person' profile based on temperament, emotional make-up, preferences and medical

Bach Flower Remedies

In 1930 at the age of 43 Dr Edward Bach gave up a thriving Harley Street practice to devote his life to natural medicine. He had become disillusioned with orthodox medicine because of what he considered to be its lack of success with chronic ailments and he was determined to develop a valid alternative based on homoeopathic principles.

As a young man he had trained at the London Homoeopathic Hospital where he learnt of the curative properties of herbs and had developed an interest in natural vaccines. It then became his ambition to develop a range of safe and simple natural cures that could be kept in every home and used without having to consult a chemist or physician.

He had been inspired to develop his system of natural remedies after attending a banquet at which he was struck by the number of people who appeared to share the same characteristics and yet were not related. It occurred to him that people might belong to generic groups, as do species of plants and animals, and that if these distinct personality types could be identified it might be possible to treat their ailments as a negative trait rather than as a random illness.

Consequently he began to prescribe 'potentised' doses of the flowering plants Impatiens and Mimulus to his patients according to the group to which they seemed to belong, rather than their symptoms. The results proved impressive. Encouraged by this he developed a range of 38 herbal remedies distilled from the essence of various flowers which became known as the Bach Flower Remedies.

How they work

The remedies treat the person rather than the illness by restoring harmony to the mind and body through a subtle empathic vibrational energy inherent in the flower. Contrary to popular belief it is not a substance in the flower that effects the cure but the energy pattern which it imprints in the solution known as the mother tincture. Detractors of the system put the efficacy of the cures down to either the brandy used in the distillation process or to the placebo effect.

Though, it is impossible to prove the effect that the essences have on the body as they do not contain physical traces of the flowers and so cannot be detected or analysed like a drug, but there is considerable anecdotal evidence to support the belief that the remedies can restore the sense of wellbeing.

Remedies are selected according to personality type, attitude and state of mind and this can be done by the patient themselves. However, it can be useful to consult a complementary therapist on which remedy to use as it is not always possible for the patient to accurately identify which personality type they belong to. It is not simply a case of recognizing that you have a problem and who or what is contributing to it, but how you react to the problem.

For example, if you believe that your family, friends or colleagues at work take you for granted then you could respond in a number of ways. You might suppress your true feelings and pretend that you don't care, you might try even harder to please them, or you might give in to negative feelings which are ultimately harmful to your own health. Each of these reactions would require a different remedy.

A therapist can also determine if more than one remedy might be necessary and whether this should be taken in conjunction with homeopathic, herbal or other treatments.

Selecting a remedy

To identify the remedy most suited to your character type ask yourself some basic questions about your childhood, your relationships, your response to criticism, your reactions to difficulties and your attitude to life in general.

In addition to 'type remedies' there are remedies for specific emotional problems. These are classified into seven distinct categories namely fear, uncertainty and indecision, apathy, loneliness, oversensitivity, depression and anxiety about the welfare of others. The most popular remedy is Rescue Remedy, which is particularly effective in moderating stress and anxiety, as well as minor cuts and even nappy rash!

Once you have chosen your remedy you can take it as frequently as you feel necessary. As a general guide the recommended dosage is four drops (of the mixed remedy) taken four times a day. These are available in ready-to-use preparations to mix in water or drop on the tongue. There is no danger in choosing the 'wrong' cure or in taking too much by mistake. They are not addictive and can be safely taken by people of all ages as well as pregnant women and even pets.

Main picture and right: The Bach Flower Remedies offer 38 herbal extracts distilled from flowers which imprint their energy pattern in the Mother tincture.

Crystals

The visionary author Aldous Huxley believed that crystals held a fascination for many people because they reminded them of the multi-faceted, vividly coloured landscapes of the inner worlds. This is not a new fascination; many of the Megalithic stone circles which our prehistoric ancestors erected at significant sites all over Europe were constructed using stones with a high mica or quartz crystal content. The peculiar characteristic of these crystals and therefore of the stone circles themselves is that they produce both ultrasound and infrasound when struck by the rays of the rising sun to produce a measurable electromagnetic energy field. Our ancestors may have tuned in to this primal tone during their ceremonial rituals to commune with the forces of nature and the inner realms.

Special properties

The idea that crystals possess peculiar properties of their own which can be harnessed for protection or healing, that they can be used to store psychic energy or to serve as a focus for the psychic's own inner vision may have a basis in the belief that the earth itself could be a giant crystal.

In the 1960s researchers working for the Russian Academy of Sciences theorized that the earth had been formed around a crystalline framework, the remains of which can still be seen in 12 vast pentagonal blocks on the surface. If this is true, the entire structure of our planet may serve as a matrix

for cosmic energy. This may account for the peculiar properties of individual crystals and explain the source of many natural disasters as well as the reason why ancient civilizations built their sacred monuments on certain sites.

Uses of crystals

1 *As an aid to developing greater psychic awareness* Take a selection of crystals that have been suitably cleansed (see right). Hold one at a time in your hand and try to sense the distinctive quality of their particular energies. People respond in different ways, but you should sense that some give off heat of varying intensity, some give out a prickly sensation, while others may trigger symbolic images showing that you are responding on an unconscious level.

2 *As a focus for divination* Forget the myth that crystal balls possess the power to reveal the future. The crystal in this form is a focus for the reader's inner vision. The image itself actually forms in the mind, but is 'seen' between the reader and the crystal, not in it.

3 *As a source of psychic protection* Purple amethysts have long been considered to be particularly effective in clearing negative energy and restoring the polarity to areas where the energy fields are imbalanced. For that reason

Left: Crystals can be used to cure plants and animals, as well as human beings.

they are often used in healing, but they are said to be equally effective in protecting property from burglars and vandals if placed at strategic points on window sills and shelves.

4 *As a source of healing energy* Recently crystal healing has become an accepted form of complementary medicine. Practitioners are divided into those who believe that the stones themselves possess healing properties and those who use crystals to store their own psychic energy for later use. In the latter case a therapist will charge the crystals by holding their hands over the crystal and directing or channeling energy from their own chakras into the stones.

Often the choice of crystal used for healing will be made by the stone's response to the patient rather than any particular properties that the crystal itself is believed to possess. A series of pendulums fashioned from suitable stones may be held over the patient's hand and their reaction will determine which will be used.

The method of application will differ according to the therapist but the usual form of treatment involves either laying the crystal on the affected area and moving it in a clockwise direction to clear the energy blockage, or laying a stone over each of the chakras and allowing the crystals to

harmonize the body.

Crystals relating to certain problems can be carried about on a necklace or set in a ring to cure minor problems such as menstrual pain, migraines or sore throats. But the patient must remember to take off the crystal at night as it is said that there is a danger that some of the stronger stones could burn a hole in the person's aura!

Cleansing your crystal

A newly acquired crystal needs to be cleansed as it may have picked up negative vibrations before coming to you. There are several cleansing methods outlined below and it is a matter of personal choice which one you use:

● Hold the crystal in one hand and say the words 'I will and command that this stone will be self-cleansing'. Repeat this and visualize the negative energy falling away from the crystal.
● Hold the crystal under cold flowing water and allow it to dry naturally in the sun or the warmth of your home.
● Immerse the crystal in salt water for several hours and allow to dry as above.
● Bury the crystal in your garden for several hours, where the magnetic energy field in the earth will cleanse it.
● Place the crystal next to a large quartz crystal cluster. Crystalline energy in the cluster will neutralize any negative energy.

Left: Our fascination with crystals may originate from unconscious memories of the inner worlds.

Spiritual healing

Spiritual healing is not the same as faith healing, which has religious connotations. With modern spiritual healing the patient does not need to believe in the potential power of the healer, nor subscribe to a particular belief system, but simply be willing to receive the infusion of energy which it is thought they soak up through a psychic connection.

Healers consider themselves to be channels for divine energy and not the source of the healing power themselves. This energy is, of course, also present in the patient and so all that the healer is doing is assisting the natural life force to stimulate the subtle energy centres of the depleted person to revitalize their own healing power.

In fact, it is the healer who needs to have faith; faith in the Eternal Spirit from whom they draw the love, light and healing power and faith in themselves and their ability to be open and clear channels for that power.

What happens during a treatment session?

The healer should begin by asking if the patient has ever had healing before and if not, explain what it involves. They should also mention that sometimes a patient can feel a little worse after a session before feeling the benefit as healing works from within, releasing negativity which needs to be 'cleared'.

Healers are obliged to ask if the patient has seen a doctor and if not, they should

Above: 17th-century healer Valentine Greatrakes curing a patient by the laying on of hands.

recommend that they do so because healers are not permitted to make diagnoses, or offer medical advice. Healing is offered as a complementary therapy and never as alternative to orthodox medicine.

The patient remains fully clothed during treatment but any spectacles should be removed. The healer will begin treatment by laying his hands on the patient's shoulders to 'tune in' and merge with their aura, or the etheric energy field. Once the empathic link is made it is not necessary for the healer to use touch at all. Massage and manipulation are

not part of the healer's practice. Some healers prefer the laying on of hands to make a strong connection, but many find it sufficient to pass their hands close to the body, concentrating on balancing the chakras and channelling energy to any specific areas that they feel drawn to.

What are the benefits?

One of the great benefits of spiritual healing is that a sensitive healer can identify the specific cause of an illness by scanning for cold spots in the etheric field, even when the illness has manifested as a physical symptom in another part of the body. Often the patient will feel heat coming from the healer's hands and they may also begin to feel warm themselves as their own energy begins to circulate more freely after the blockage has been dissolved.

The whole process can take as little as ten minutes or as much as an hour and there is no limit to the amount of treatment that a patient can have, but they should consider that the majority of healers give their time freely. It is rare for a healer to charge a fee and those who do generally ask for a nominal donation for their favourite charity.

The central concept behind spiritual healing is that much of what we interpret as pain, lack of energy or disease is the physical symptom of a spiritual or emotional sickness resulting from an energy block (literally disease) in the etheric body.

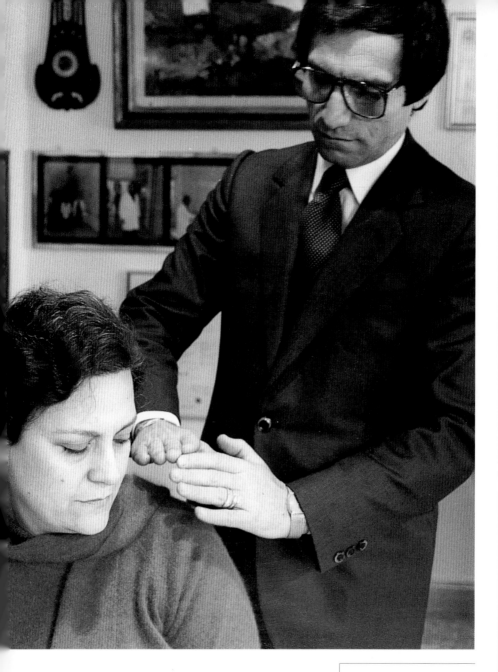

The pain, strain and physical deterioration are often real, but when a healer works on the emotional or mental source of the sickness, rather than the symptom, complete cures can normally be effected without recourse to powerful drugs or surgery.

Of course, it is not necessary for patients to accept this explanation, or even to have blind faith in the potentially miraculous powers of the healer. Those who have been helped and are healthier and happier than before their treatment can thank any god or power source they like.

It is advisable to choose a healer who is registered with one of the official associations because they will have trained under supervision and be practising under strict guidelines.

Above: In modern spiritual healing many practitioners do not feel the need to touch the patient, but instead transfer vital energy to the aura from where it is absorbed into the patient's system.

Betty Shine

Betty Shine, the British medium whom the tabloid press have dubbed 'the world's number one healer', has testimonials from thousands of people around the world attesting to the power of spiritual healing. In many cases Betty did not even have to 'lay hands' on her patients, but appears to have affected her miracle cures through what is known as absent healing. This involves the healer 'channelling' the healing energy from the universal life force through their hands while focusing on a letter or a photograph of the person needing treatment.

Through her best-selling books Mind to Mind, Mind Magic and Mind Waves and her numerous television appearances Betty has introduced millions to the apparently unlimited healing powers of the mind and the latent paranormal powers that we all share.

Early psychic abilities
From an early age she discovered her innate ability to pass effortlessly between this world and the next. As a young child she claimed she experienced the exhilaration of astral flight and found comfort from nightly visitations by shadowy spirit entities who used to walk through her bedroom and then disappear through the outside wall.

But her mother was against anything psychic on principle

and so Betty suppressed her abilities until at the age of 46, after a career as an opera singer and mineral therapist, the repressed energies started to threaten her health. In desperation she turned to a medium for guidance and was told that her destiny was to be a world renowned psychic and healer – a destiny she was at first very reluctant to both believe and to pursue.

The power of miracles
'To be a great healer or medium you've got to know that power is there for the asking,' she says. 'You must be positive and have faith that miracles will happen. Why should your patient or the person who has asked for a reading have faith. They haven't had the miracle yet! So, open yourself up. Fun and laughter and a feeling for those you are trying to help will release all these energies naturally. Have you noticed how often you see the Dalai Lama and his followers laughing at what seems to be a private joke? It's because they've found the meaning of life which is happiness.'

Betty has little patience with the New Age gurus who insist on regular and elaborate rituals for opening and closing the chakras (the energy vortexes in the etheric body), contacting their 'inner child', and healing their bruised egos and deflated spirits.

'All that New Age stuff is a load of nonsense,' she says. 'They put so much emphasis on opening the chakras that people get obsessed about these invisible forces and they get themselves in a real mess. I know because I've had to give healing to the casualties. The chakras are dangerous centres of energy to unleash if you don't know how to control them properly. You can easily get them tangled up by trying too hard and end up with your energy centres unbalanced.'

'Through psychic sight I've actually seen the mind energy pressing down on people's heads instead of opening out simply because they were trying too damn hard to make it work. The mind is the most incredible gift we have been given and yet so many people ask God to do all the work. They blame fate for their misfortunes and don't take responsibility for their own development and good fortune.'

Betty believes that the only people who should be exploring the potential powerhouse of energy in the chakras are dedicated Buddhists and highly developed individuals working under the guidance of a real master. She maintains that if we are in reasonable health the chakras will open and close naturally as we go about our daily lives, opening to higher emotions such as love and compassion and closing when

Above: Medium and healer Betty Shine has introduced millions to the unlimited healing power of the mind.

we immerse ourselves in mundane chores.

'We are all psychic,' she comments. 'But knowing that you are opens the mind to the cosmic energies that will come in and do the job. Whatever you give out joins like thoughts out there in the Universal Mind and will multiply and come back at you. And if your thoughts are negative they will invariably come back to you when you are at your lowest ebb. That's why negative thinking people appear to get caught up in the momentum of an ever descending spiral of what the ordinary person would perceive as 'bad luck'. But they have created their own condition. They blame the whole bloody world instead of themselves. When you recognise that you can break free and take control of your own life.'

Psychic surgery

Miracle cures are no longer the exclusive preserve of those with blind faith in saints and holy relics. Spiritual healers and psychic surgeons from South America to the suburbs of South London are now said to be working miracles on a daily basis using just the heat of the energy emitting from their hands. They are also performing painless operations without the use of anaesthetics.

With the aid of their spirit guides (who were invariably doctors themselves in a previous incarnation) spiritual healers claim to be able to manipulate matter by raising its level of vibration so that they can work on the matrix of energy which we call the etheric body, rather than the flesh.

This concept is similar to the Hindu and Buddhist belief that what we perceive to be solid matter is in fact countless microscopic particles held together by the etheric body to give the illusion of form. Science is rapidly moving towards this conclusion and it is hoped that when it does officially recognize this 'greater reality' complementary therapies and orthodox medicine will come together to create a holistic system of healthcare.

Psychic surgeons

But the 50 or so patients who come from all over the world each day to the clinic of Stephen Turoff, England's most celebrated psychic surgeon, can not wait for the medical establishment to acknowledge the potential benefits of spiritual healing. Many are suffering severe and debilitating pain. Some have been diagnosed with terminal cancer with no hope of remission, while others claim that orthodox medicine has failed them. Stephen is often their last hope and their journey to his small suburban clinic in Chelmsford, Essex, is more like a pilgrimage than a medical appointment.

Patients speak of feeling nothing but the pressure of his fingers and the blunt edge of a blade when Stephen makes his incision, of seeing pastel lights absorbed into their bodies, of towels and sheets turning pink in his presence and of sacred ash materializing on the photographs of Indian avatar Sai Baba and the other saints and avatars who apparently bless his work.

Using spirit guides

What they will also tell you is that it is not Stephen himself who affects the cures, but his spirit guides and helpers who use this genial giant as their instrument. The most prominent of these is Dr Kahn, a Viennese surgeon who died at the age of 70 in 1912 and whose identity and existence have subsequently been verified by independent sources.

It all sounds too incredible to be true, and yet sceptics find their doubts dissolve after watching the remarkable transformation that takes place

Right: Celebrated psychic surgeon, Stephen Turoff, treats a patient surrounded by pictures of the Hindu saints who are said to bless his work.

when the spirit of the diminutive Viennese surgeon takes over Stephen's body. At first Stephen's face darkens to the wrinkled features of a much older man and then his imposing tall, large frame visibly shrinks requiring him to roll his trouser legs up several turns so that they don't trail across the floor. He also assumes Dr Kahn's pronounced limp and gruff German accent.

'A deep trance is like going to sleep,' says Stephen. 'I don't remember anything about what has happened [...] The human helpers and patients tell

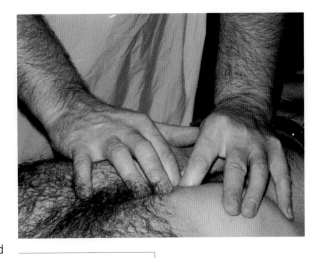

Above: Psychic surgeons manipulate psychical matter to operate on the etheric body, where the sourse of dis-ease lies.

me what Dr Kahn did whilst I was gone.'

Stephen welcomes witnesses if they are friends or relatives of the patient and even allows his operations to be filmed. He has found that some patients need corroboration before they can believe what they have seen. It is simply too incredible for the human brain to accept.

Miraculous cures

Stephen's 'miracle cures' inevitably attracted the attention of the media who couldn't resist the temptation to play up the sensationalist aspects, but they also prompted a serious scientific study. In 1992, after five years of close examination of Stephen's methods and results its author, Doctor Linda Chard, concluded, 'We know that Stephen is not masquerading. I have seen a doctor, dead to the earth plane, perform operations that defy normal scientific interpretation [...] My understanding of what Dr Kahn does when de-materializing diseased tissue is that by altering the sub-atomic energy within the cellular structure of the tissue he is able to disperse it into recyclable matter.'

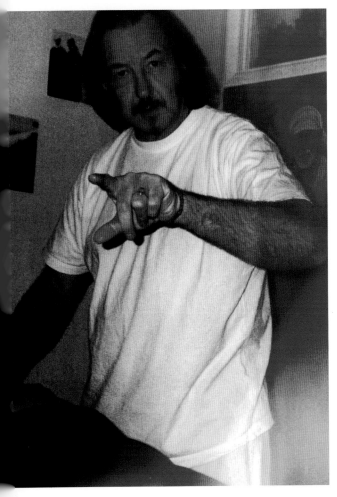

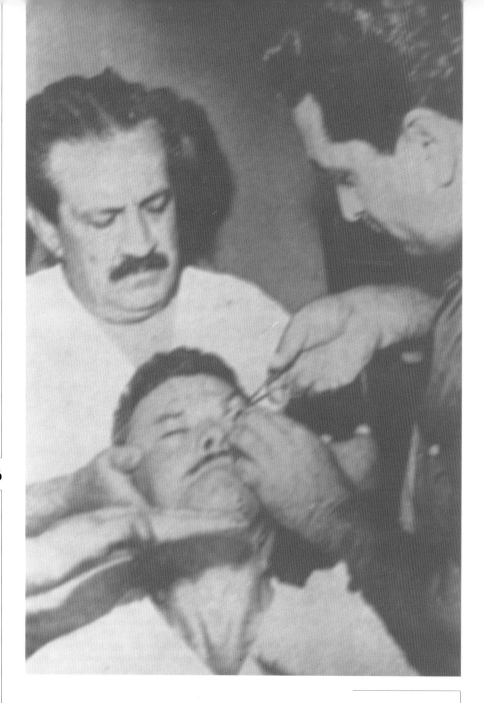

Above: A Filipino surgeon performs a delicate eye operation without anaesthetic.

There are hundreds of psychic surgeons practising around the world, many of them in Brazil and the Philippines where the phenomenon is more widely accepted and not subject to rigorous regulations as it is in Europe and America.

Genuine healers

Unfortunately, not all of the healers are genuine, but the remarkable cures affected by the Brazilian healer known only as Arigo stood up to close scrutiny when examined by an American doctor and psychic researcher, Henry Puharich.

In 1963 Dr Puharich visited Arigo's clinic in Belo Horizonte with a cameraman and caught several operations on film – including his own! While the camera rolled Arigo operated on the American investigator without anaesthetic or antiseptic. With just two cuts from a borrowed penknife he removed a tumour that

Puharich wasn't even aware he had and sealed the wound with nothing more than a Band-Aid. Although the cut was not even cleaned it healed completely in just three days.

After his impromptu operation in Brazil the once sceptical Dr Puharich described the experience which had convinced him of the power of psychic surgery.

'In spite of being perfectly conscious I had not felt any pain [...] Yet there was the incision in my arm, which was bleeding, and there was the tumour [...] the film showed that the entire operation had lasted five seconds. Arigo had made two strokes with the knife [...] The skin had split wide open and the tumour was clearly visible. Arigo then squeezed the tumour as one might squeeze a boil, and the tumour popped out.'

Dr Puharich was forced to conclude that, 'Our nice modern equipment proved that genuine healing took place under bizarre conditions and unbelievable circumstances. Clearly, we have a lot of research ahead of us.'

Accurate diagnosis
Medical experts were also mystified by the Brazilian's ability to make accurate diagnoses without a close examination and to estimate his patient's blood pressure without instruments. Arigo was also renowned for prescribing specialized drugs of which he could have had no prior conscious knowledge, having had no medical training of any kind.

When asked how he performed such feats without medical knowledge or training,

Arigo blithely stated that he listened to a voice in his right ear which identified itself as belonging to the spirit of a dead German medical student.

Promoting spiritual healing
The American movie actress and New Age devotee Shirley Maclaine has done much to promote the phenomenon of spiritual healing among the general public through her chat show appearances, a series of bestselling autobiographies, and public demonstrations of psychic surgery in which she was both patient and assistant.

In her sixth book, Going Within, she recalls the time when she decided to prove the existence of psychic surgery for herself, having been intrigued by watching videos of operations shot in the Philippines. 'I had made enough movies with remarkable special effects to doubt what I was seeing on tape,' she remarked. 'I needed to see it in person. And I needed to keep an open mind.'

Observing psychic operations
When she learned that the world famous Filipino healer Alex Orbito was coming to Las Vegas as part of an extensive tour of America she asked for a private appointment for herself and a female friend.

As Maclaine watched in disbelief Orbito, a slim, immaculately dressed, youthful-looking man with a beguiling smile kneaded the bare skin of her friend's torso above the waist until it seemed to transmute into another form of almost plastic-like matter and separated, allowing

his hands to disappear into the body!

'There was blood,' Maclaine confessed, 'and there was a sloshing sound as his hands searched around for something near her heart.'

While Orbito was operating Maclaine's friend was groaning with pleasure from what she later said was the therapeutic heat of his hands.

'His hands were literally inside her abdomen up to his wrists!' recalled Maclaine with ill-concealed astonishment. 'I slapped my own face to ensure I wasn't dreaming [...] His hands were actually in there! Both of them.'

After removing several clots of what appeared to be blood Orbito withdrew his hands, the gaping 'wound' sealed itself and the woman climbed off the bed, smiling broadly and obviously exhilarated by the experience.

Having observed Orbito at work and then submitting to a series of similar 'operations' herself, MacLaine subsequently organized a series of public demonstrations during which Orbito extracted teeth and removed tumours, including one from a patient's brain. Then, to Maclaine's astonishment, Orbito gave her a unique opportunity to experience what it was like to perform psychic surgery. He took her right hand in his and plunged it into a patient's abdomen up to the wrist. 'I felt absolutely nothing physical,' she recalled. 'In fact, the feeling had a dreamlike quality to it. It was as though I had plunged my hand into a warm mist.'

bibliography

Bonewitz, R., *The Cosmic Crystal Spiral*. Shaftesbury, 1987.

Bradbury, W., *Into the Unknown*. London, 1983.

Bradford, N., *The Hamlyn Encyclopedia of Complementary Health*. London, 1996.

Campbell, E. and Brennan J.H., *Dictionary of Mind, Body and Spirit*. London, 1994.

Cheun, Master Lam Kam, *The Way of Healing*. London, 1999.

Chuen, Master Lam Kam, *Step-by-Step Tai Chi*. London, 1994.

Eason, C.A., *Complete Guide to Divination*. London, 1998.

Gawain, S., *Creative Visualisation*. California, 1978.

Halevi, S., *The Work of the Kabbalist*. Bath, 1994.

Hay, L.L., *You Can Heal Your Life*. London, 1988.

Holroyd, S., *Mysteries of the Inner Self*. London, 1981.

Lovelock, J., *Gaia: the Practical Science of Planetary Medicine*. London, 1991.

Moolenburgh, Dr H.C., *Meetings with Angels*. Saffron Walden,1992.

Redfield, J., *The Celestine Prophecy*. London, 1995.

Reid, H., *The Book of Soft Martial Arts*. London, 1994

Rinpoche, S., *The Tibetan Book of Living and Dying*. London, 1993.

Roland, P., *The Complete Guide to Dreams*. London 1999.

Roland, P., *Piatkus Guide to Kabbalah*. London, 1999.

Roland, P., *Piatkus Guide to Angels*. London, 1999.

Roland, P., *Revelations – the Wisdom of the Ages*. London, 1995.

Shine, B., *Mind to Mind*. London, 1996.

Shine, B., *Mind Magic*. London, 1996.

Skelton, R., *The Practice of Witchcraft Today*. London, 1992.

Solomon, G., *Stephen Turoff – Psychic Surgery*. London, 1997.

Watson, N., *Practical Solitary Magic*. York Beach, 1996.

Watts, A., *Seeds of Genius*. Shaftesbury, 1997.

West, J.A., *The Case for Astrology*. London, 1992.

Wilson, C., *The Occult*. London, 1979.

Wilson, C., *Mysteries*. London, 1979.

index

Page numbers in italics refer to picture captions.

Acknowledgements

AKG, LONDON, Front cover left. BRIDGEMAN ART LIBRARY, LONDON, NEW YORK/ British Library Front cover right. SCIENCE PHOTO LIBRARY/David Gifford Front cover bottom centre. MARY EVANS PICTURE LIBRARY Front cover centre back. IMAGE SELECT Front cover top. IMAGES COLOUR PICTURE LIBRARY LIMITED/ Charles Walker Collection Front flap. FORTEAN PICTURE LIBRARY back jacket. WERNER FORMAN ARCHIVE/Statens Historika Museet, Stockholm Back flap.

AKG, LONDON, 65, 82, 102-103/Erich Lessing 12.
AMORC, Rosicrucian Order 15.
THE DR EDWARD BACH CENTRE 176-177.
BRIDGEMAN ART LIBRARY, LONDON/NEW YORK/Agnew & Sons, London, UK. 81//British Library, London, UK 20/By Courtesy of the Board of Trustees of the Victoria & Albert Museum 100-101/Galleria degli Uffizi, Florence, Italy 102/Huntingdon Park, Los Angeles, California, USA/Dinodia Picture Agency, Bombay, India 90-91 Background/Museo de Bellas Artes, Bilbao, Spain, Index 101/Private collection 111
/Private Collection/Dinodia Picture Agency, Bombay, India 29, 139/Warburg Institute, London, UK 17.
BUBBLES/LoisJoy Thurston 178, 179.
CORBIS UK LTD 52, 64-65 Background, 69, 70-71, 118-119 Background, 131, 148/Dave Bartruff 21
/Morton Beebe 8 Top Right/Yann Arthus-Bertrand 32-33 Background/Marilyn Bridges 48-49 background/Owen Franken 2-3/Michelle Garrett 172/Todd Gipstein 173/Hulton-Deutsch Collection 116-117, 120-121/Galen Rowell 146-147/Michael St Maur Sheil 49/Adam Woolfitt 35.
DANBURY HEALING CLINIC 185/Stephen Turoff 184-185.
COURTESY OF THE DICKEN'S HOUSE MUSEUM 130.
MARY EVANS PICTURE LIBRARY, 5 Top Left, 14, 60, 76, 78, 84, 98, 99, 110, 122, 125, 127, 155, 156, 157/Collection of Guy Lyon Playfair 186/Harry Price Collection, University of London 106-107 Background/Institution of Civil Engineers 6-7 Background/John Cutten Collection 104.
FORTEAN PICTURE LIBRARY, 5 Top Centre, 8 Top Left, 25, 38-39, 112-113, 128-129/Klaus Aarsleff 6, 27, 133/Paul Broadhurst 4 Top Centre/Kevin Carlyon 36, 37/Dr Elmar R. Gruber 47, 181/Paul Broadhurst 40-41/Philip Panton 70, 94-95/Guy Lyon Playfair 107.
SALLY AND RICHARD GREENHILL 119, 148-149 Background/Richard Greenhill 5 Top Right, 136-137 Background, 137, 165/Sally Greenhill 162/Sam Greenhill 164-165 Background.
OCTOPUS PUBLISHING GROUP LTD. 12-13 Background, 66, 68-69 Background, 72-73, 72-73 Background, 74, 74-75 Background, 77, 78-79 Background, 108-109, 123, 170, 171/Courtesy of Hahneman Museum/Peter Chadwick 175/Bob Gibbons 51/Peter Myers 159, 160, 160-161 Background/Simon Smith 166-167 Background/John Webb 67/W Adams-Lingwood 167.
HULTON GETTY PICTURE COLLECTION facing half-title, 16-17 Background, 83, 88-89 Background.
IMAGE BANK/Todd Davidson 97/Clint Eley 96-97 Background/Grant V. Faint 54-55 Background
/Piecework Productions 30-31 Background/Regine M. 28-29 Background/Shoji Yoshida 154-155 Background.
IMAGE SELECT 34-35 Background/Roy Curtis half title, 44-45 Background, 46-47 Background/Chris Fairclough 143/Ann Ronan 52-53.
IMAGES COLOUR LIBRARY LIMITED 141 Top/Thrity Enigineer 140.
MONKWELL 152-153.
REX FEATURES 50, 56-57/Francois Gauthier 30/Curtis Knapp 58.
THE RONALD GRANT ARCHIVE 24-25 Background, 39.
SCIENCE PHOTO LIBRARY, 104-105/Bsip Boucharlat 115/Latin Stock/Oscar Burriel 4 Top Right/Simon Fraser 22, 60-61 Background/David Gifford 169/G. Hadjo 140 Bottom/Mehau Kulyk 43/Latin Stock, Oscar Burriel 62-63/Royal Observatory, Edinburth 22-23 Background/Francoise Sauze 117/Sheila Terry 180
/Geoff Tompkinson 135.
TONY STONE IMAGES/Dale Durfee 144-145/Ernst Haus 55/James Harrington 96/Zigy Kaluzny 162-163
/Vera Storman 4-5 Background.
TIBET IMAGES/Anders H. Anderson 93/Catriona Bass 86-87/Diane Barker 86/Ian Cumming Front Endpaper, Back Endpaper, 4 Top Left, 10-11, 89/Mike Ford 26/Mani Lama 92-93.
TRANSWORLD PUBLISHERS/Betty Shine 183.
WERNER FORMAN ARCHIVE 9, 45, 91/National Museum, Denmark 33/Private Collection facing acknowledgements.

192